A CREATIVE GUIDE TO

CROCHET

JAN EATON

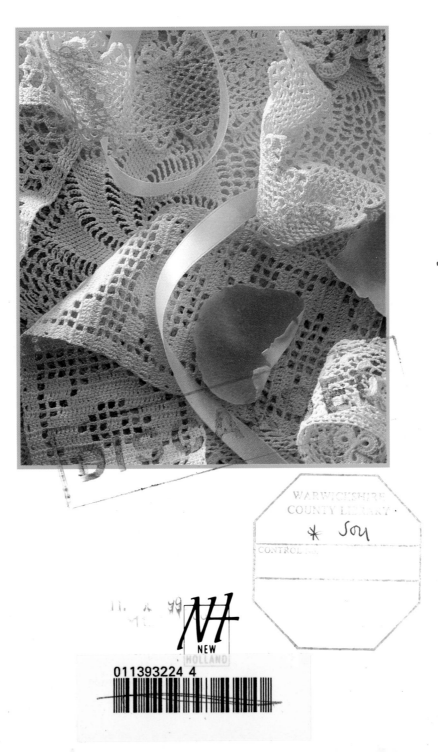

NEW
HOLLAND

First published in the UK in 1994 by
New Holland (Publishers) Ltd
37 Connaught Street, London W2 2AZ

ISBN 1 85368 289 6

Editor Coral Walker
Assistant editor Sue Thraves
Art director Jane Forster
Photographer Steve Tanner
Illustrators Stephen Dew and Coral Mula

The author would like to thank the following:
Shelagh Hollingworth for her invaluable work writing and
charting patterns from historical pieces of crochet
Annette Claxton and Jane Easson-Brown for their help and
encouragement
DMC Creative World for supplying sample threads

Typeset by Ace Filmsetting Ltd, Frome, Somerset
Reproduction by Scantrans Pte Ltd, Singapore
Printed in Malaysia by Times Publishing Group

The Craft of Crochet   4

A look back in time. Filet Crochet. Crochet today.

Practical Skills   11

Choosing and using yarns. Crochet hooks and other equipment. Calculating yarn requirements. Tension. Crochet stitches. Finishing off. Working filet crochet. How to follow a written pattern. How to follow a charted pattern. Using the Pattern Library. Finishing techniques. Caring for and storing crochet lace.

Projects in Crochet   30

Crystal and Silver Tablecloth. Country Cottage Bedspread. Butterfly Tablecloth. Hearts and Diamonds Bedspread. Snowflake Traycloth. Scalloped Shelf Edgings. Roses Pincushions. Crochet Bags. Lavender Bags. Christmas Stars.

Pattern Library   64

Edgings. Borders. All-over stitch patterns. Filet crochet motifs, insertions and alphabets.

Useful Suppliers   78

Bibliography   79

Glossary   79

Index   80

The craft of crochet

The craft of crochet has been practised for centuries to make garments and furnishings for both the home and the church. Crochet is known throughout the world: it is worked in countries from Europe to South America and China to the Middle East, using a variety of materials, styles and patterns to produce textures ranging from gossamer-fine, ornate lace to sturdy, woollen fabrics.

The basic stitches of crochet lace are simple to work and you will quickly become familiar with the various techniques which are involved. Whether making a length of intricate edging in fine cotton yarn to edge a snowy white tablecloth or working a pretty bag in thick yarn, the stitches and techniques you will use are exactly the same. Always use the best quality yarn you can buy and look after the finished item to make sure that you can use and enjoy your crochet lace throughout the years.

A LOOK BACK IN TIME

Crochet, like knitting, is a looped fabric made from a continuous length of yarn. Unlike knitting – where a multiple of stitches are worked on two needles at any one time – crochet uses a short hook on which one stitch is worked at a time. The term 'crochet' is thought to come from the French word *croc*, meaning a hook, but its origins are impossible to trace with any accuracy as very few early pieces exist today. Unlike pottery, metalwork and even glass, the various forms of textile crafts, particularly those made for every-day domestic use and wear, have not survived in great numbers over the centuries due to the impermanent nature of the fibres used.

Some schools of thought believe that the origins of crochet and knitting were the same, possibly invented in the Middle East, and that the techniques are linked by a type of crochet called Tunisian crochet which is worked on a long hook in a similar way to knitting. Others suggest that the two crafts developed independently. Whatever the exact origins, the early fragments of crochet which are known to exist have been found in places right across the world from Europe to Africa, China to Turkey and the United States to South America.

Crochet can be worked to have two very different appearances. Using fine yarn and fine hooks, the resulting fabric is light, open and can compete on its own terms with the finest bobbin and needle-made laces. Crochet can also be worked in thick woollen yarn on large hooks to produce a heavy, densely-worked fabric. This heavier crochet appears to have been the most widespread of the two types.

The Chinese made three-dimensional, sculptured crochet dolls, African tribes worked ceremonial headgear for their chiefs and in Scotland, warm caps and cloaks were fashioned for shepherds to wear when tending their sheep in the fields. In some parts of Scotland, crochet is also known as 'shepherd's knitting'.

Crochet lace probably originated in Italy during the sixteenth century. Worked extensively during this period by nuns to make wonderfully ornate church vestments and trimmings, crochet was also known as 'nun's lace'. Italian crochet lace was worked in very fine cotton yarn using tiny ivory or bone hooks, and knowledge of the technique spread gradually through the Roman Catholic world across Europe to Spain and Ireland.

By the nineteenth century, crochet lace was used to trim garments and linens in the wealthiest households. The techniques were liberated from the confines of the European church largely due to the enthusiasm of a French émigré, Eleanore Riego de la Branchardière, who settled in Ireland

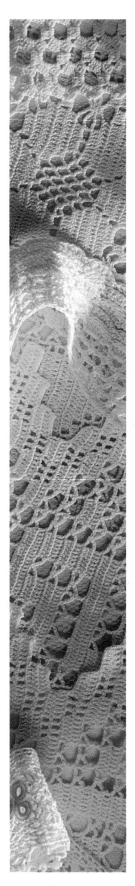

and was fascinated by the fine crochet laces made by the nuns in Dublin convents. She learnt how to work this very intricate crochet lace and invented many new and interesting stitches and patterns which she published in the secular magazine she founded called *The Needle*.

In the mid 1840s when the potato crop, the staple food of the Irish, failed and potatoes rotted in fields all over Ireland, many women and children were able to earn money by making crochet lace as well as doing other kinds of 'fancy needlework' including knitting and embroidery. They were taught the necessary skills and organized by nuns, who supplied the materials and marketed many of the finished products. Irish crochet lace of this period was of a very high quality and imitated the appearance of expensive, handmade European laces.

A distinctive type of fine crochet with relief motifs of roses and shamrocks worked on a delicate lattice background began to be worked in Ireland during this period, primarily as the result of two home industry schemes set up for peasant women by Mrs Porter in Carrickmacross and Mrs Hand in Clones. Often called Irish crochet, this type of crochet lace is also known by its places of origin, as Carrickmacross lace and Clones lace.

Irish crochet patterned with leaf, rose and shamrock motifs is still worked today and is used to make decorative insertions and edgings for garments and linens as well as complete items such as bedspreads and tablecloths.

Examples of antique Irish lace command high prices when they come up for auction – this is usually a rare occurrence as most fine pieces are greatly prized and handed down from generation to generation. Many of the Irish peasant women who worked fine crochet lace emigrated to the United States with their families to make a new life away from the poverty of their famine-stricken homeland and they passed on the techniques, stitches and designs they had learned.

During the second half of the nineteenth century, crochet lace was in vogue in Britain and the colonies – Queen Victoria accepted gifts of Irish crochet lace to trim her gowns and the popularity of the new type of lace spread rapidly across Europe from court to court. Queen Victoria actually learned to crochet and was often seen working crochet lace patterns in public. Books of crochet patterns were published in Europe and the United States and designs appeared in all the women's magazines of the day from the British *Woman's Magazine* to the American *Godey's Lady's Book*.

Weldon's Practical Crochet was a series of practical magazines published in England around 1895 and available by yearly subscription 'post free to any Part of the World'. The variety of patterns is breathtaking – from 'How to Crochet 47 Useful Articles for Ladies, Gentlemen and Children', including slippers, quilt squares, shawls, a boy's cricketing cap and a cosy antimacassar, to 'New and Original Designs for Mantel Valances, Brackets, Borders for Sideboard Cloths, Piano Covers etc' worked in coloured yarn over pre-formed moulds.

FILET CROCHET

During this peak of popularity, the most sought after designs were for a crochet lace technique called 'filet crochet' using areas of light and shade to create a realistic or abstract design. Today, filet crochet is still worked extensively throughout Europe and the United States.

A versatile form of crochet, filet crochet is based on a regular, square grid or network. It is extremely simple to work, as the technique uses only the basic chain, double crochet and treble stitches. The grid serves as the background for geometric and figurative designs which are created by 'filling in' some of the spaces of the grid with blocks of treble stitches to create areas of light and shade. Lacets and bars are variations on the grid which create a more open, lacy surface.

The true filet lace is an expensive, hand-knotted net, made with a netting shuttle, which has designs darned on it using a needle and thread. Filet crochet, originally worked as an inexpensive substitute for this time consuming, hand-made lace, gives a similar, slightly coarser result, but the work requires less skill and dexterity than true filet lacemaking.

Filet crochet designs are expressed in chart form and originally ranged from simple repeated geometric motifs to large landscapes and pictorial scenes, complete with human figures, birds, flowers, fruit and animals.

Traditionally, this type of crochet was worked with fine hooks in fine white or ivory cotton and linen yarns to produce complex, large scale pictures often depicting a scene from the Classics or the Scriptures. As simple, bold lettering is also effective in filet crochet, many designs incorporated a text such as The Lord's Prayer or a religious maxim or educational verse similar to those found in embroidered samplers of the period.

CROCHET TODAY

Crochet lace is currently enjoying a revival and people are rediscovering the pleasures of creating a fine piece of lace by hand. The techniques are simple to master, and the craft requires little in the way of equipment apart from hooks and yarn. Once you have found a brand of hooks you are comfortable with, buy a complete set, preferably with a case so the required size is always to hand.

Some of the crochet lace pieces in this book, including the butterfly tablecloth (page 39) and hearts and diamonds bedspread (page 42) have been in my family for many years. My maternal grandmother, who taught me how to crochet as a small child, worked large pieces of fine filet crochet to make curtains and edge tablecloths well into her seventies. Specific yarns, hook sizes and tension have not been quoted, but the patterns have been written and charted for you to recreate these heirlooms of your own. The yarn thickness hook size chart opposite will help you select your materials.

The remaining projects have been designed specially for this book, particularly with beginners in mind. The two country rose pincushions on page 51 make the ideal introduction to filet crochet, while the hexagon shape lavender bags (page 59) give the novice useful practice at working crochet in rounds. Each project is graded with a degree-of-difficulty symbol so you can tell at a glance which projects are suitable for your level of ability and skill.

The pattern library on pages 64-77 contains over 20 more stitch patterns for crochet lace including shell and openwork stitches for making shawls and wraps, a selection of motifs which can be worked and joined together in a variety of ways, and a selection of charts for filet crochet from small pictorial designs to alphabets for personalizing your household linen. Each section in the pattern library is introduced with suggestions for using specific stitches.

NOTE FOR LEFT-HANDED READERS

When following the diagrams for working crochet stitches and techniques, prop the book up in front of a large mirror so the diagrams are reflected in reverse (ie left-handed) form.

NOTES FOR NORTH AMERICAN READERS

Both metric and imperial measurements are used throughout the book and there is a hook conversion chart below. However, there are a few differences in crochet terminology and yarn names between the UK and the US. These are:

UK terms	US terms
Double crochet (dc)	Single crochet (sc)
Half treble (htr)	Half double crochet (hdc)
Treble (tr)	Double crochet (dc)
Double treble (dtr)	Treble crochet (tr)
Tension	Gauge

UK yarn names	US yarn names
3 ply	Lightweight
4 ply	Fingering or mediumweight
Double knitting	Sport
Aran weight	Worsted or fisherman
Double-double or chunky	Heavyweight or bulky

Chart for crochet yarn weight/hook size combinations

No 60 cotton	0.6 mm
No 40 cotton	0.75 mm–1 mm
No 30 cotton	1 mm–1.25 mm
No 20 cotton	1.25 mm–1.5 mm
No 10 cotton	1.5 mm–1.75 mm
4 ply	2 mm–3.5 mm
Double knitting	3.5 mm–4.5 mm
Aran	5 mm–6 mm
Chunky	6 mm–7 mm

Crochet Hook Conversion Chart

International Metric	British Old sizes (Aero) WOOL	COTTON	American
0.6		7	14
0.75		6½	12
1		5½	10
1.25		4½	8
1.5	16	3½	7
1.75	15	2½	4
2	14	1½	0
2.5	12	0	B
3	10	3/0	C
3.5	9		E
4	8		F
4.5	7		G
5	6		H
5.5	5		–
6	4		I
7	2		K

Practical Skills

CHOOSING AND USING YARNS

There is a wide variety of yarns available which can be used to make crochet lace. Traditionally, this was worked in very fine cotton, linen or wool yarns but today almost any type of yarn with a smooth surface is acceptable. The weight of yarns you can use varies from the finest mercerized No 60 cotton to double knitting yarn. However, fluffy, hairy yarns such as mohair and textured, knobbly yarns are not successful; a lace stitch pattern worked in mohair will be indistinct, while one in textured yarn will pull out of shape owing to the knobs in the yarn.

Yarn is usually sold ready-wound into balls of a specific size and the amount contained in each ball is quoted by weight rather than by length. The weight is given in grams or ounces – the most common ball sizes are 25 g or 50 g (1 oz or 2 oz) – and the length of yarn in the ball will vary from yarn to yarn depending on thickness. Occasionally, yarn is sold in coiled hanks or skeins and this must be wound by hand into balls before you begin to crochet. Fine cotton yarn is sold in a small, flattened ball wound round a card or plastic and usually labelled with length as well as weight.

Pure wool and wool/synthetic mixtures are formed by twisting together a number of strands or 'plies'. The finished yarns are available in several weights, from fine 2 ply to heavy double-double knitting weight (also known as chunky). Use the quoted ply as a general guide to the thickness of the yarn, as yarn measurements are not standard from spinner to spinner and the thickness will vary according to the degree of twist as well as the fibre composition.

Thick cotton yarns are also available in two plies, 4 ply and double knitting. Many of the finer cotton yarns available in the shops are labelled as crochet cotton, and are particularly good for working crochet lace as these yarns are mercerized, making them smooth and very strong with a slightly glossy surface. The thickness of crochet yarns is quoted in a series of graded numbers, from the coarsest (No 3) to the finest (No 60).

For the beginner, double knitting wool or a wool/synthetic yarn is ideal for practising stitches, patterns and techniques. Wool retains a certain amount of stretch and 'give' when it is spun into a yarn and this makes stitches easier to work. Begin by using a 4 mm crochet hook with this weight of yarn. When you have become familiar with using the wool yarn, change to a smooth cotton yarn of about the same thickness and work your stitches in this, again using a 4 mm hook. Cotton yarn is harder on the fingers than wool and has very little 'give' in it, but lace stitch patterns show up well. When you feel confident handling this weight of yarn and size of hook, move on to finer yarns and hooks. The chart on page 11 gives information about hook sizes and suggests yarn weight/hook size combinations.

Each ball of yarn is wrapped in a paper band (called a ball band) which gives you lots of useful information about the yarn. As well as fibre composition and the weight of the ball, it will also show the colour and dye lot number, symbols for washing and pressing and often a range of suitable hook sizes plus tension details. International yarn care symbols are shown above.

The dye lot number on the ball band is particularly important as when the yarn is dyed in batches there are often subtle

variations in colour between lots. Although this difference may not be apparent when you compare balls of yarn in your hand, it will probably show as a shade variation when the yarn is made up and may look unsightly. Always use yarn from the same dye lot for a single project.

Make sure you keep a ball band for each piece of crochet lace you work. Keep it in a small polythene 'grip-top' bag with any left-over yarn and label the bag with details of the item you have made, including hook size. You will then be able to refer to the washing instructions and have the correct yarn ready to make any necessary repairs.

CROCHET HOOKS AND OTHER EQUIPMENT

Standard crochet hooks are made from steel, aluminium or plastic in a wide range of sizes. Steel hooks are the finest and they are used for working with fine crochet cottons, while aluminium and plastic hooks can be used for all types of thicker yarns. Today, the old numerical system has been

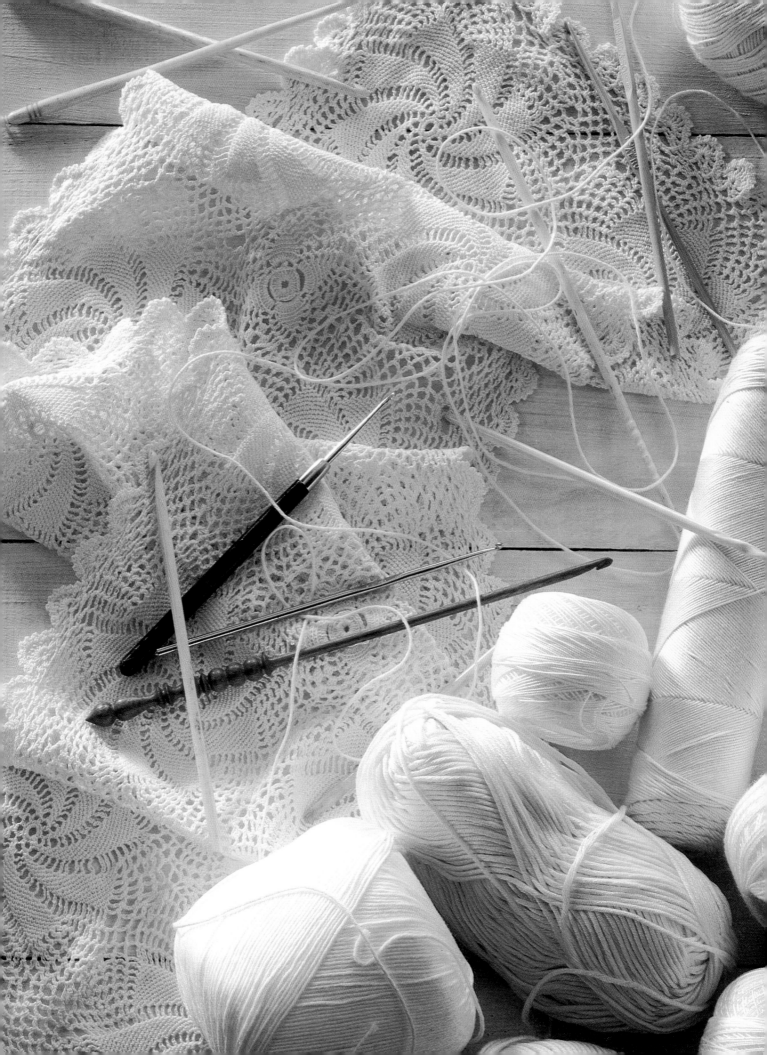

replaced by metric sizes and the hooks are marked with the size halfway down the shaft. The chart on page 11 gives the conversions from old to new hook sizes, as well as American sizes. Steel hook sizes range from 0.6 mm to 1.75 mm, aluminium from 2 mm to 7 mm and plastic from 8 mm to 15 mm.

As well as the standard hooks, steel hooks with chunky plastic handles are available. The sizes are identical to those of standard steel hooks, but the plastic handles make the hooks easier to grip and use if you have difficulty holding a fine hook. Continental wooden hooks are also available in a small range of sizes from 3.5 mm to 6.5 mm.

Row counter
A useful piece of equipment, the row counter is actually a knitting accessory which tells you the number of the row you are working; but one is just as useful when working crochet. The counter is a short cylinder with a numbered dial which is usually slipped on to one knitting needle close to the knob. When working crochet, keep the counter close by the pattern and turn the dial at the end of every row.

Markers
Split loops made from brightly coloured plastic can be clipped on to a crochet stitch to mark a place in the pattern. Short lengths of contrasting coloured yarn or bright embroidery cottons can be tied to a stitch to mark it instead.

Tapestry needles
Tapestry (also called yarn) needles have long eyes and blunt points. Keep a selection of sizes handy and use them when finishing thread ends and for sewing pieces of crochet lace together. Use ordinary sewing needles when applying a crochet edging, border or insertion to a piece of fabric.

Other equipment
Keep a bag or workbox handy containing general sewing equipment including sharp scissors, stainless steel pins with glass or plastic heads, a good quality dressmakers' tape measure, a selection of sewing needles and threads.

CALCULATING YARN REQUIREMENTS

As many of the crochet lace projects in this book were made in the early part of the century, the yarns used cannot be identified and are probably no longer available, so reliable guidelines to yarn quantities cannot be given. Keep in mind that the smaller projects, for example the country rose pincushions (page 51) and lavender bags (page 59), require less than 1 ball of yarn.

For the larger projects, such as the scalloped shelf edgings on page 48, the best way to calculate your yarn requirement is to crochet up one complete ball of your chosen yarn in the stitch pattern you wish to work, after first making small samples to check the compatibility of yarn and hook. At the end of the ball, pin out and block (page 26) your piece of crochet and let it dry completely. Next, check how many pattern repeats one ball of yarn has made and divide this figure into the total number of repeats you need. For example, if one ball of yarn makes 8 repeats of the pattern and you need to work 40 repeats in total, to make the desired length of edging you will need to buy 5 balls of yarn for each edging strip. Always buy slightly more yarn than you think you will need – odd balls can always be used up to make small items or whole balls of surplus yarn may sometimes be returned for a refund. Check with your supplier before purchase.

TENSION

When working a piece of crochet you must make sure that the fabric you produce is neither too loose and floppy nor too tightly worked and stiff. It is also important that the hook size you have selected is compatible with the weight of yarn you are using. This is called tension (also known as gauge) and is usually quoted as a number of rows and stitches over a given area of crochet fabric, usually 10 cm (4 in) square. When making a garment, correct tension is vital to ensure that the garment is the correct size when finished. Garment patterns include a tension guideline stating the number of rows and stitches which must be achieved. With items of home furnishing, the size is less crucial and the effect and handling quality of the finished crochet fabric is more important.

Because many different yarn weights can be used to make the projects in the book, specific yarns, hook sizes and tension cannot be quoted with any accuracy. The pattern instructions suggest a type of yarn, for example double knitting weight cotton, but you could substitute a finer yarn if you prefer. Apply commonsense when choosing yarn for a project – obviously the Christmas stars on page 62 would look less dainty and attractive worked in thick yarn, while the crochet bags on page 54 would be impractical worked in fine yarn on a large hook as they would not keep their shape when used. The chart on page 11 suggests various hook and yarn weight combinations and you can use this chart as a basis for your choice. Remember also that many yarns give a range of suitable hook sizes on the ball band.

Instead of working to a specific stitch and row count when working the crochet lace projects, make several small sample pieces with your chosen yarn and hook to check the results you will get before beginning to make the real thing. Crochet lace should be light and holey, but the crochet fabric should not be so loose that the stitches will pull out of shape when the article is handled. Remember that tension is a very individual thing – two people working with exactly the same pattern, yarn and hook will always produce slightly different results. As a general rule, if your samples are too tight and stiff, change to a larger size of crochet hook, while if the fabric is too loose and floppy, use a smaller size hook.

CROCHET STITCHES
Chain stitch (ch)

1 Begin with a slip knot on the hook, then wrap the yarn over the hook as shown. Unless otherwise stated, always wrap the yarn round the hook in this way.

2 Draw the yarn through to make a new loop without pulling the previous loop too tight.

Slip stitch (ss)

Insert the hook in the work, wrap the yarn over the hook, then draw the yarn through both the work and the loop on the hook in one movement.

Double crochet (dc)

1 Insert the hook into the second chain from the hook (one turning chain made), wrap the yarn over the hook and draw the yarn through the work only so that there are now two loops on the hook.

2 Wrap the yarn over the hook again and draw the yarn through both loops on the hook.

Half treble (htr)

1 Wrap the yarn over the hook and insert the hook into the third chain from the hook (two turning chains made).

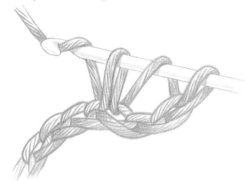

2 Wrap the yarn over the hook and draw the yarn through the work only so that there are now three loops on the hook, wrap the yarn over the hook again and draw through all three loops on the hook.

Treble (tr)

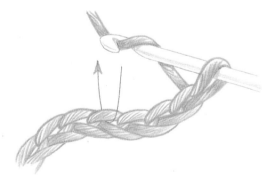

1 Wrap the yarn over the hook and insert the hook into the fourth chain from the hook (three turning chains made).

2 Wrap the yarn over the hook and draw the yarn through the work only so that there are now three loops on the hook.

3 Wrap the yarn over the hook and draw the yarn through the first two loops on the hook, wrap the yarn over the hook and draw the yarn through the remaining two loops on the hook.

To work two treble stitches together (tr2tog)

Work a treble, but omit the last part so that two loops remain on the hook. Work the second treble in the same way so that two loops remain on the hook. To complete, wrap the yarn over the hook and draw through all the loops on the hook.

Double treble (dtr)

1 Wrap the yarn over the hook twice and insert the hook into the fifth chain from the hook (four turning chains made).

2 Wrap the yarn over the hook and draw it through the work only so that there are now four loops on the hook.

3 Wrap the yarn over the hook again and draw it through the first two loops on the hook, leaving three loops on the hook.

4 Wrap the yarn over the hook and draw it through the next two loops only, wrap the yarn over the hook again and draw it through the remaining two loops on the hook.

Crossed double treble
The stitches forming a crossed double treble are worked in the same way as an ordinary double treble (above) but the two stitches are crossed, one behind the other.

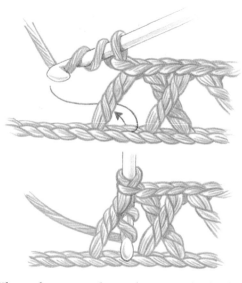

When the second stitch is worked, the hook is taken behind the first stitch before being inserted into the work.

MAKING A FOUNDATION CHAIN
Crochet stitch patterns are worked on a row of chain stitches, called the foundation chain or row. The number of chains to work for each pattern is given in the relevant instructions, but remember to work the stitches loosely and also to count the number of stitches correctly.

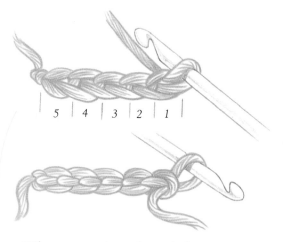

When counting the stitches as you make them, do not count the slip loop as a stitch, instead count each chain as you work it. When the foundation chain is finished, count the stitches again, this time counting the slip loop but ignoring the loop on the hook. Check that you are looking at the front of the chain when counting. The diagram shows both the front and back of the chain.

When the foundation chain is finished, turn and work the first pattern row into the chains as follows:

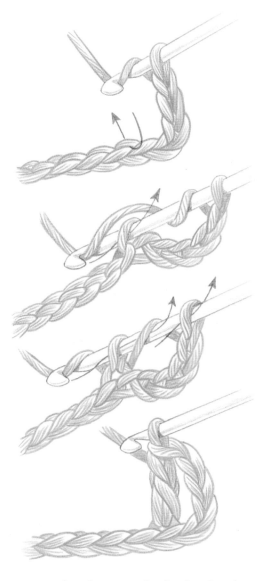

Turn the chain so the back of it faces you. Work the first row according to the pattern, inserting the hook into the centre of the chain as shown. This method makes a neat edge along the bottom of your work. The diagram shows a row of trebles being worked into the chain.

TURNING CHAINS

When working crochet in rows or rounds, you will need to work a specific number of extra chains at the beginning of each row or round in order to bring the hook up to the correct height for the stitch you are using. This is called a turning chain (starting chain when working in rounds) and the diagram shows the correct number of chains to work for each crochet stitch.

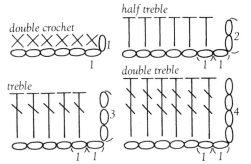

Usually, the turning chain (except in the case of double crochet where the single turning chain is ignored) is counted as the first stitch of the row. The number of chains to work is stated in each pattern in this book.

WORKING IN ROUNDS

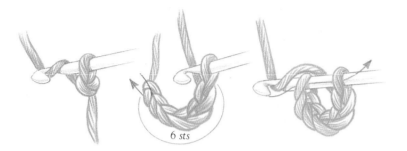

6 sts

To work crochet in rounds when making a square, round or shaped motif, begin by making a length of chain stitches and join the length into a ring. Count the stitches in the same way as for a straight foundation chain (above), and when you have worked the required number, join it into a ring with a slip stitch (see diagram).

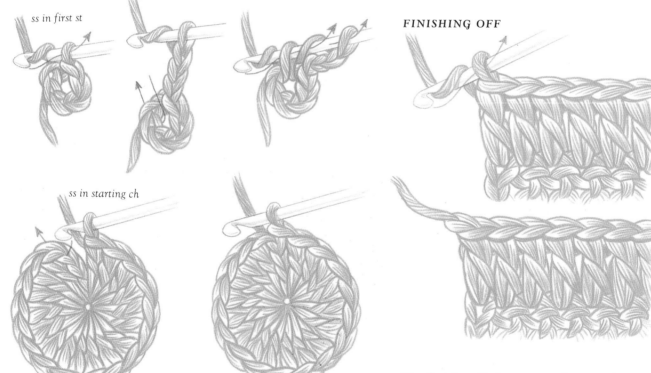

ss in first st

ss in starting ch

To begin the second round, work the correct number of starting chains (the diagram shows three starting chains as the round is worked in trebles). Continue the round following the pattern instruc-

tions, working each stitch into the centre of the ring, as shown. At the end of the round, join the first and last stitches with a slip stitch. Work subsequent rounds in the same way, beginning each one with the correct number of starting chain.

JOINING A NEW BALL OF YARN

Join a new ball of yarn at any point, making sure there is at least 10 cm (4 in) of the old ball left unworked. Knot the two ends together close to the work, then proceed in pattern as before, working the knot through to the wrong side when the join is reached. After you have finished the piece of crochet, go back and carefully undo any knots, then fasten off the ends securely with a tapestry needle as described on page 26.

FINISHING OFF

To finish off the yarn when a piece of crochet has been completed, make one chain then cut off the yarn, leaving a piece about 5 cm (2 in) long. Draw the end of the yarn through the chain and tighten gently. Fasten off the yarn end with a tapestry needle (page 26).

WORKING FILET CROCHET

Filet crochet is always worked from a chart and these are very easy to read as they show the pattern as it will appear from the right side of the work. Follow the numbered sequence at the sides of the chart, working from side to side and reading odd-numbered rows from right to left and even-numbered rows from left to right.

Each open square on a filet crochet chart represents one space on the grid. The space is formed by two trebles separated by two chains. When the chart square is filled with a dot, the two chains are replaced by two trebles to form a solid block of four stitches. Two blocks together on the chart are filled by seven treble stitches, three blocks by ten stitches and so on.

On some filet crochet charts, the blocks are indicated by crosses or solid squares rather than dots.

The foundation row is not shown on a filet crochet chart. Instead, to calculate the number of stitches needed in the foundation row, you will need to multiply the number of squares across the chart by three and add one. For example, for a charted design with 35 squares across, make a foundation row 106 chains long (35 × 3 + 1). You will also need to remember to add the appropriate number of turning chains, depending on whether the first chart row begins with a space or a block (see 'How to begin', below).

Lacets and bars are variations on the basic grid structure of blocks and spaces, and the variations create a pretty, more lacy effect.

A lacet or a bar is worked over two squares on the chart. On the chart, a lacet is shown as a 'V' shape and a bar as a horizontal line. Lacets are always worked in conjunction with bars, although bars may be used alone.

How to begin:

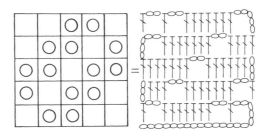

1 Begin by making the foundation chain as described above and start to follow the chart from the bottom right-hand corner. When the first square is a space, add four turning chains and work the first treble into the eighth chain from the hook. Continue working spaces and blocks along the row from right to left.

2 When the first square is a block, add two turning chains and work the first treble into the fourth chain from the hook, then work one treble into each of the next two chains and continue along the row.

To continue:

At the end of the row, turn the work and follow the second row on the chart, reading from left to right. Work spaces and blocks at the beginning and end of the second and subsequent rows as follows.

TO WORK A SPACE OVER A SPACE on the previous row, work 5ch (counts as 1tr and 2ch) – at the beginning of the row, miss first st and 2ch, 1tr into next tr, then continue working the spaces and blocks directly from the chart. At the end of the row, finish with 1tr into last tr, 2ch, miss 2ch, 1tr into 3rd of 5ch, turn.

TO WORK A SPACE OVER A BLOCK on the previous row, work 5ch (counts as 1tr and 2ch) – at the beginning of the row, miss first 3 sts, 1tr into next tr, then continue working spaces and blocks from the chart. Over the last 4 stitches at the end of the row, work 1tr into next tr, 2ch, miss 2tr, 1tr into top of 3ch, turn.

TO WORK A BLOCK OVER A SPACE on the previous row, work 3ch (counts as 1tr) – at the beginning of the row, miss 1st, 1tr into each of next 2ch, 1tr into next tr, then continue working spaces and blocks from the chart. At the end of the row, finish with 1tr into last tr, 1tr into each of next 3 ch of turning ch, turn.

TO WORK A BLOCK OVER A BLOCK on the previous row, work 3ch (counts as 1tr) – at the beginning of the row, miss 1st, 1tr into each of next 3tr, then continue working spaces and blocks from the chart. At the end of the row, finish with 1tr into each of last 3tr, 1tr into top of 3ch, turn.

Working lacets and bars

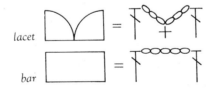

working lacets and bars in a pattern

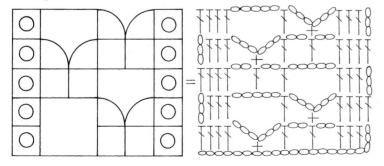

Lacets form a 'V' shape in the basic grid. A bar is usually worked on the row above to restore the depth and rectangular shape of the grid, but can also be worked over a bar in the previous row to create a double space in the grid.

TO FORM A LACET: work 3ch, miss 2 sts on the previous row, 1dc into next stitch on previous row, 3ch, miss 2 sts, 1tr into next tr on previous row.

TO FORM A BAR: work 5ch, miss next lacet on previous row (or next two spaces), 1tr into next tr on previous row.

TO RETURN TO THE BASIC GRID above a bar on the previous row, work 2ch, 1tr into 3rd of 5ch, 2ch, 1tr into next tr.

Crochet abbreviations

ch chain
ss slip stitch
dc double crochet
htr half treble
tr treble
tr2tog work two treble stitches together
tr4tog work four treble stitches together
dtr double treble
st(s) stitch(es)
rep repeat
rem remaining
cont continue
alt alternate
beg beginning
foll following
patt pattern
sp space
* asterisk denotes that you must repeat a sequence of stitches from that point
[] the sequence of stitches enclosed inside square brackets must be worked as instructed
() round brackets contain extra information to help you, not instructions

FOLLOWING A WRITTEN PATTERN

Crochet patterns are written in a logical way, even though at first sight the instructions can appear rather complicated. The most important thing to remember when following a pattern is to check that you start off with the correct number of chains in the foundation row or ring, and then work through *exactly* as stated.

Begin by reading the pattern before you start to crochet. As well as instructions, it will contain information about materials, measurements and finishing off the item. Although some instructions or details may not be clear on the first reading, the technique involved will be much easier to grasp once you begin work.

Crochet abbreviations are standard, see opposite; any special abbreviations are explained on the relevant pattern.

Asterisks

In order to make written patterns shorter and avoid tedious repetition, asterisks are used to indicate which sections of the instructions have to be repeated across a row. For example, an instruction such as '1tr into next st, * 3ch, miss 3 sts, 1tr into each of next 3 sts; rep from * to end' means that you begin the row by working one treble into the next stitch on the previous row, then work repeats of three chain, miss the next three stitches on the previous row, work one treble into each of the next three stitches right across the row until you reach the other side.

You will also find some instructions which tell you how to work any stitches remaining after the last complete repeat is worked. These will be similar to this instruction: 'rep from * to end, ending with 1dc into each of last 2ch, 3ch, turn'. In this case, after the last repeat has been worked, work one double crochet into each of the last two chain then work three chain and turn.

Square brackets

Square brackets fulfil a similar function to asterisks and both may be used in the same pattern row. Always repeat the sequence of stitches shown inside the square brackets as instructed before proceeding to the next instruction in the row. For example, a row reading '1tr into first st, * 2ch, miss 2 sts, [1tr, 3ch, 1tr] into next st; rep from * to end' instructs you to work one treble into the first stitch on the previous row, work repeats of two chain, miss two stitches on the previous row, work one treble, three chain and one treble into the next stitch on the previous row until you reach the end of the row.

Round brackets

Round brackets do not contain working instructions. Instead, they give extra information which you may find helpful; for example, by indicating the number of trebles made in a particular row by the time you reach the end.

Repeats

Each stitch pattern is written or charted using a specific number of pattern rows and the sequence is repeated until the work is the correct length. A simple pattern, such as the shelf edgings on page 48, is six rows long, while the deep edging on the crystal and silver tablecloth (page 32) requires 24 rows of crochet to work one complete pattern repeat. In some of the more complex projects – the butterfly tablecloth (page 39), for example – specific sections of the pattern are repeated. Where this is the case, the project instructions will tell you exactly which sections of the chart are to be repeated.

When working a complicated stitch pattern, always make a note of exactly which row you are working. Use a row counter or write the row number in a notebook with a pencil as it's very easy to forget where you are when your crochet session gets interrupted by the doorbell or a telephone call. Avoid the temptation to use a pen when making notes as ink is rather messy and can be very difficult to remove from light-coloured yarn.

FOLLOWING A CHARTED PATTERN

Many people prefer working from a chart rather than from written instructions. Although a charted pattern still contains some written instructions, the stitch pattern is expressed in visual form. Traditionally, British crochet patterns, with the exception of those for filet crochet, have been written rather than charted. However, there is now a strong movement towards the charted pattern which is used almost exclusively in other European countries. Charts also solve the problem of translating a long, complicated stitch pattern from one language to another.

To use a crochet chart, first familiarize yourself with the symbols and their meanings. These are explained in a key at the side of the chart. Each symbol represents a single instruction, such as double crochet or treble and indicates exactly where to work the stitch. Follow the numerical sequence shown on the chart whether you are working in rounds or rows.

In the same way as when using written instructions, keep a note of which row you are working at any one time using a row counter or notepad and pencil.

Crochet symbols

The chart shows the main symbols used in crochet charts. A key is also given beside each project and pattern library chart.

USING THE PATTERN LIBRARY

The pattern library pages give both written and charted instructions for a wide variety of crochet lace patterns. Filet crochet patterns are given as charts only.

Many of these stitch patterns can be substituted for project designs, particularly the edging and border patterns. A selection of square motifs are given on page 66 which would make a lovely bedspread – work the motifs and join them together in the same way as the country cottage bedspread on page 36. The small filet crochet pictorial designs on page 75 can be substituted for the country roses charts on page 51.

To use the pattern library instructions for crochet lace worked in rows, begin by working the correct number of stitches in the foundation chain. For an edging, border or insertion, this number is given at the top of each pattern. Other patterns give you the correct number of chains needed to work one complete pattern repeat. For example, the first line of the large shell pattern on page 74 tells you to 'work a multiple of 10ch plus 2'. This means that the total number of chains to work so the pattern will be correct when finished must be divisible by 10, and you must also add two extra chains. So your foundation row could have say 62 chains (6 × 10 + 2) or 102 (10 × 10 + 2) and the pattern would be correct in either case. When working in rounds, the number of chain needed to make the ring is given with each pattern.

Making your own chart for filet crochet

You can easily adapt a simple squared chart (from Fairisle knitting or cross stitch, for example) for filet crochet by plotting the design on graph paper. Decide which areas are to be solid and fill these in with dots on the graph paper. The unmarked squares left indicate the grid background. One important point to remember, however, is that when working filet crochet from a square chart, the resulting piece of crochet is not likely to be perfectly square.

o Chain *ch*

● Slip stitch *ss*

+ Double crochet *dc*

T Half treble *htr*

⳨ Treble *tr*

⳨ Double treble *dtr*

FINISHING TECHNIQUES

FINISHING OFF THREAD ENDS

Thread the end of the yarn through a tapestry needle and weave the point of the needle through several stitches on the wrong side of the work for at least 2.5 cm (1 in). Pull the needle and yarn through and cut off the yarn end.

PINNING OUT AND BLOCKING

This process is essential for bringing out the delicate patterns in crochet lace and it can be used safely with either cotton, wool or wool/synthetic mixture yarns as no heat is applied. Although blocking may seem rather a lengthy and tedious process, the time invested will be well spent.

To pin out and block crochet lace you will need a large piece of blockboard or chipboard covered with thick cork floor tiles, brown paper, drawing pins, a sheet of polythene, stainless steel pins with glass or plastic heads and a small plant sprayer filled with cold water.

Draw the outline of the piece on to the brown paper with a pencil – for a border draw two parallel lines, for a circular piece, draw radiating lines from the centre corresponding with the number of motifs in the pattern, and for a square or hexagonal motif draw the shape to the correct size. Pin the brown paper on to the board with drawing pins and cover it with the polythene sheet.

Spray the piece of crochet lightly with water and pin it out over the drawn shape using stainless steel pins. Don't be tempted to use ordinary dressmaking pins as these will rust and leave unsightly brown stains on the yarn. Adjust the pins until the crochet lace is stretched evenly, then spray with water once again, this time more heavily. Allow the crochet to dry completely at room temperature before removing the pins (this may take more than a day, depending on the yarn thickness). When you remove the pins, the crochet fabric will retain the shape in which it dried. When blocking a border or edging, you will need to work in several sections, letting the work dry before moving on to the next section.

JOINING MOTIFS

After pinning and blocking all the crochet motifs to the same size, join them together in one of the following ways:

Oversew (see diagram) square motifs together using the same yarn. Oversewing makes a very flat seam once it is opened out and pressed, unlike alternative methods which create an unsightly ridge.

Lay out the motifs to be joined in the correct order on a flat surface with the right side of each motif facing upwards. Working in horizontal lines, oversew the motifs together as shown, inserting the needle into a single loop of corresponding stitches. Secure the thread carefully at the beginning and end of the stitching.

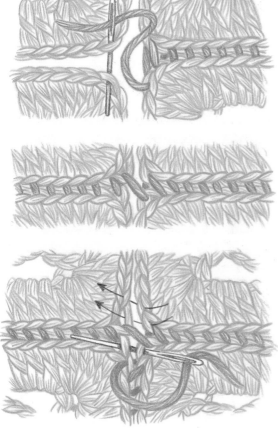

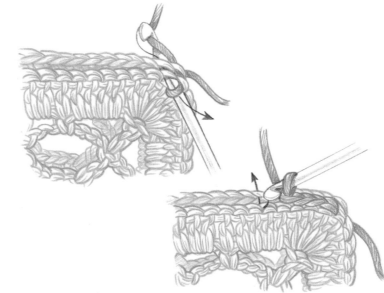

Place two motifs together with right sides facing and the edges to be joined aligning. Work a row of slip stitch as shown in the diagram, securing the thread at the beginning and end of the square. Repeat this with further motifs until you have a strip of joined motifs which is the required length. Make as many strips as you require, then join the strips together in the same way, taking care to match up the short seams across the strips.

Join lacy shaped motifs, like the snow-flake shapes on page 45, by slip stitching them together at regular points round the edge of the motif. Complete the first motif, then work the second motif until you reach the last round. Following the pattern instructions, work the last round until you reach the point where the motifs are to be joined, place them together with right sides upwards and then join with a slip stitch as shown in the first diagram.

When all the horizontal seams have been stitched, repeat the oversewing to stitch the vertical seams. To make a stronger seam, you can insert the needle through both loops of corresponding stitches.

Alternatively, join square motifs together by **slip stitching** them together stitch by stitch.

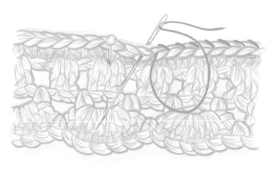

Using a tapestry needle and the same yarn that you used for the crochet, oversew (see diagram) the layers together. If you have used a very heavy yarn for the crochet, you will get a neater seam if you use a thinner thread, but don't be tempted to use sewing cotton as this will not be strong enough to take the weight of the crochet.

Crochet lace edgings and borders to fabric

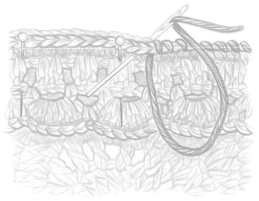

Continue in pattern, joining the two motifs together at the points indicated.

APPLYING BORDERS, EDGINGS AND INSERTIONS

A border to a crochet bedspread
Place the crochet border on top of the bedspread with right sides facing and straight edges aligning. Pin in place, distributing the length of the border evenly and gathering it slightly at each corner so that it will lie flat without pulling. Use long pins with glass or plastic heads so the pinheads will not pull through the crochet fabric.

Position the edging or border on top of the hemmed edge of the fabric with right sides facing and straight edges aligning. Make sure that the edging is evenly distributed and pin in place using glass-headed pins. Using a sewing needle and matching sewing cotton, stitch the crochet and fabric together using oversewing stitches (see diagram). Make small, neat stitches and take care not to pull the thread too tightly. When applying edging to a corner, gather the crochet slightly so that the edging will lie flat when stitched in position.

Adding insertions

Crochet lace insertions are applied between two pieces of fabric and are often used in conjunction with an edging or border.

Pin the top of the insertion to the first piece of fabric with right sides facing and proceed as above. Then pin the lower edge of the insertion to the second piece of fabric and sew in the same way.

Caring and storing

Follow the cleaning and pressing instructions on the ball band for the particular yarn you are using – a list of the international care symbols found on ball bands is given below. If the yarn you have used is machine-washable, put the item into a clean white pillowcase to prevent stretching during the machine cycle.

When not in use, store crochet lace wrapped in white, acid-free tissue paper in a cool and dry place. When folding a large item, pad the folds with tissue paper to prevent hard creases forming or, better still, roll it right-side out round a cardboard tube between layers of tissue paper.

With a little care, you can use and enjoy the crochet lace items you have made for years to come. Follow these guidelines:

○ Always wash crochet lace before it gets really soiled, taking prompt action to remove stains as soon as they occur, particularly on table-linen.

○ Repair holes and split seams as soon as possible to prevent further damage.

○ Keep items out of direct sunlight, especially during summer, as the sunlight will not only cause colours to fade, but will eventually weaken the fibres.

Starching crochet lace

Articles trimmed with crochet lace edgings benefit from being starched after laundering. Choose a stiff-finish starch for small items such as placemats and table runners and a soft-finish one for tablecloths and other items which will be draped or folded in use. The best method is to use soluble starch mixed with water. Dip the article into the starch solution, squeeze out the moisture, allow the item to dry then press with a hot iron.

Spray starch works well with small items, but take care when ironing as it can scorch when using a very hot iron.

Type of care	Dry cleaning	Washing	Bleaching	Drying	Ironing
Fairly easy care	(A) Use any dry-cleaning fluid	6/40° Machine-wash at stated temperature	(Cl) Chlorine (household) bleach may be used	Can be tumble dried	High setting – hot
Treat carefully	(P) Use perchlorethylene or white spirit only	30° Hand wash at stated temperature		Dry on a line	Medium setting – warm
Handle with great care	(F) Use white spirit only	Wash by hand only		Allow to drip dry	Low setting – cool
Do not use treatment shown	Must not be dry-cleaned	Must not be washed	Do not use household bleach	Do not hang – lay flat	Must not be ironed

Projects
in crochet

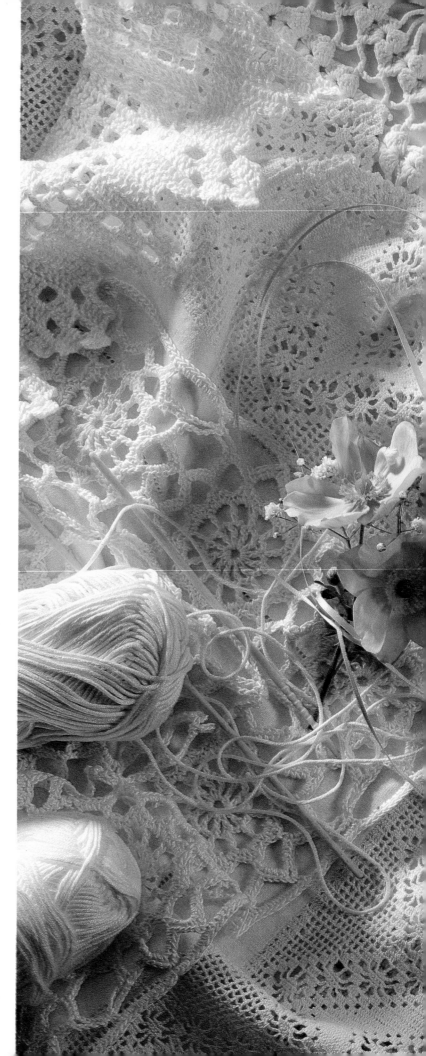

When selecting a project to make,
choose one which reflects your
present level of skill. Read right
through the instructions before you
begin to crochet. You will also find
it useful to work up one or more
sample pieces to check the effect of
your chosen yarn and hook.
The following projects are aimed at
people with varying levels of skill,
from outright beginners to more
experienced crochet enthusiasts.
You'll find a symbol with one, two
or three crochet hooks at the start of
each project. One hook indicates a
very simple design, two indicates
intermediate level and three hooks
are for more advanced projects
which should only be attempted by
a reader with considerable
experience and patience.

CRYSTAL AND SILVER TABLECLOTH

This attractive tablecloth is edged with a deep crochet border which has a pretty zigzag edge. The border is worked in fine cotton yarn and will take a considerable time to finish, but straight strips of the same design could be worked in a thicker yarn to decorate fluffy white towels for your bathroom. To do this, repeat the 24-row design from the chart until the strip is the correct length, making sure that both ends match. Stitch the strip to one short edge of the towel using matching sewing thread.

Materials
White fine crochet cotton, No 40
White cotton or linen fabric
Steel crochet hook 0.6 mm
White sewing thread
Sewing needle
Pins

Measurements
The original edging measures 15cm (6 in) deep. Work sufficient pattern repeats to make a border of the desired size to fit your table. When buying fabric, remember to allow a hem allowance of 1.5 cm (⅝ in) all round.

A deep border worked in fine cotton yarn edges this white linen tablecloth. Although the crochet is time-consuming to complete when using such fine yarn, the effect is exquisitely delicate and lacy.

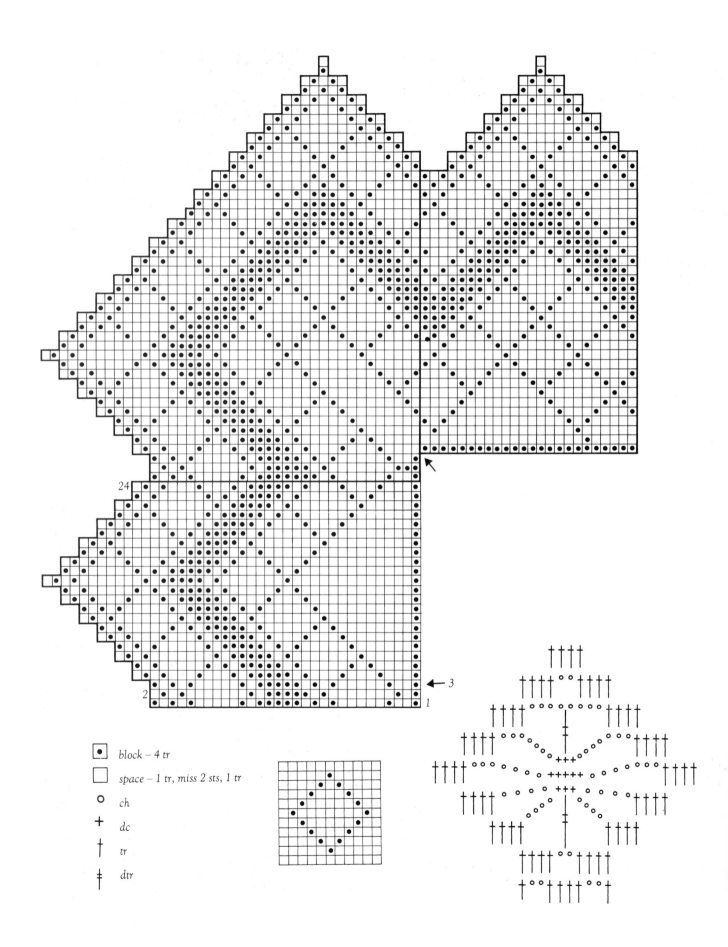

24

2

1

3

• block – 4 tr

□ space – 1 tr, miss 2 sts, 1 tr

o ch

+ dc

† tr

‡ dtr

Abbreviations

A full list of crochet abbreviations is given on page 22.

To work filet crochet, see page 21.

Working the border

FOUNDATION CHAIN Work 87ch.

ROW 1 1tr into 4th ch from hook, 1tr into each of next 2ch, [2ch, miss 2ch, 1tr into next ch] twice, 1tr into each of next 3ch, * 4ch, miss 4ch, 1dc into each of next 3ch, miss 4ch, 1tr into each of next 4ch, 2ch, miss 2ch, 1tr into each of next 4ch *, 2ch, miss 2ch, 1tr into each of next 16ch, 2ch, miss 2ch, 1tr into each of next 4ch; rep from * to *, 2ch, miss 2ch, 1tr into each of last 4ch, turn.

ROW 2 5ch, miss 2tr, 1tr into next tr, 2tr into next tr, 2ch, miss 2tr, * 1tr into next tr, 2tr into sp, 1tr into next tr, 6ch, miss 3tr, 1dc into ch before 3dc, 1dc into each of next 3dc, 1dc into ch after 3dc, 6ch, miss 3tr, 1tr into next tr *, 2tr into sp, 1tr into next tr, 2ch, miss 2tr, 1tr into each of next 13tr, 2tr into sp, 1tr into next tr, 2ch, miss 2tr; rep from * to *, 2tr into sp, 1tr into next tr, 2ch, 1tr into each of next 3tr, 1tr into top of 3ch, turn.

Continue in pattern from chart until 24 rows have been completed. Repeat the 24 rows for the length of edging required until a corner is reached. Work to end within the heavy line. Fasten off.

Rejoin at inner corner arrow. Continue in pattern working over row-ends. When work is completed, oversew top of last row to foundation chain. Fasten off.

Making up the tablecloth

1 Sew in the ends. Pin out the border a section at a time following the illustrated instructions given on page 26. Spray with water and allow to dry completely before removing the pins.

2 Pin the border on to the fabric to check the fit and carefully cut away any surplus, remembering to leave a 1.5 cm (⅝ in) hem allowance round the edge. Remove the pins. Pin and tack a narrow double hem round the cloth and machine stitch or hem neatly by hand. Press the hem well on the wrong side.

3 Pin the border round the cloth, taking care to keep the points evenly spaced along each side. Using small, neat stitches, oversew the crochet border to the fabric. Press lightly on the wrong side with a warm iron.

COUNTRY COTTAGE BEDSPREAD

Thick white cotton yarn combined with a quick-to-work motif pattern creates a stunningly simple bedspread with a country feel. The perfect accessory for stripped pine furniture, the bedspread is worked in squares which contrast lacy and solid areas made from double crochet and double treble stitches. To show the motif pattern to full advantage, lay the bedspread over coloured bedlinen, choosing blue, deep crimson, green or old gold. Instructions and charts for alternative square motifs are given in the pattern library on page 66.

Materials
White double knitting weight
cotton yarn
3.5 mm crochet hook
Tapestry needle size 22 or 24
Pins

Measurements
Each motif measures approximately 20 cm (8 in) square. You will need to make 63 complete motifs for the single size bedspread shown in the picture. To make a larger bedspread simply add more strips of motifs until your work reaches the desired size.

Abbreviations
A full list of crochet abbreviations is given on page 22. To work crossed double treble stitches, see page 18.

Working the motif
Make 8ch and join with ss to form a ring.

ROUND 1 12dc into ring, ss into first dc. On all subsequent rounds, work into the back loop of the stitch on the previous round.

ROUND 2 4ch (counts as 1dtr), * 7ch, 1dtr into same st as previous dtr, 1dtr into each of next 3dc; rep from * three times more, omitting dtr at end of last rep, join with ss.

ROUND 3 1dc into dtr, 1dc into each of 3ch, * 2dc into next ch, 1dc into each of 3ch, 1dc into each of 4dtr, 1dc into each of 3ch; rep from * three times more, omitting last dc at end of last rep, ss into first dc.

ROUND 4 4ch (counts as 1dtr), 1dtr into each of next 4dc, * 7ch, 1dtr into each of next 12dc; rep from * three times more, ending last rep 7dtr instead of 12dtr, join with ss.

ROUND 5 1dc into each of 5dtr, 1dc into each of 3ch, * 2dc into next ch, 1dc into each of next 3ch, 1dc into each of next 12dtr, 1dc into each of next 3ch; rep from * three times more, ending last rep 1dc into each of 5dtr, join with ss.

ROUND 6 4ch (counts as 1dtr), 1dtr into each of next 8dc, * 8ch, 1dtr into each of next 20dc; rep from * three times more, ending last rep 11dtr instead of 20dtr, join with ss.

ROUND 7 1dc into each dtr and ch to end, ss into first dc.

ROUND 8 4ch (counts as 1dtr), cross 2dtr, 1dtr into same st as first of the crossed

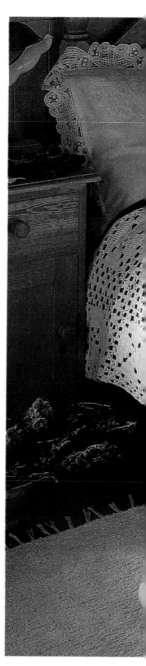

This beautiful country-style bedspread is worked in a mixture of double crochet and double treble stitches to create contrasting squares in solid and lacy patterns.

dtr, * 3ch, miss 3dc, 1dtr into next dc, cross 2dtr, 1dtr into same st as first of the crossed dtr, 8ch, 1dtr into same st as previous dtr, [cross 2dtr, 1dtr into same st as first of crossed dtr, 3ch, miss 3dc, 1dtr into next dc] twice, cross 2dtr, 1dtr into same st as first of crossed dtr; rep from * twice more, 3ch, miss 3dc, 1dtr into next dc, cross 2dtr, 1dtr into same st as first of crossed dtr, 8ch, 1dtr into same st as previous dtr, rep instructions in brackets, twice, joining with ss instead of last dtr.

ROUND 9 4ch (counts as 1dtr), work 1dtr on each dtr, with crossed dtr and 3ch loops alternating with 8th round, two joined dtr with 8ch at each corner.

ROUND 10 Rep round 9. Fasten off.

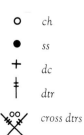

o	*ch*
●	*ss*
+	*dc*
‡	*dtr*
✕	*cross dtrs*

Making up the bedspread
1 Sew in the ends. Pin out each motif following the illustrated instructions given on page 26, making sure that all the motifs are of identical size. Spray with water and allow them to dry completely before removing pins.
2 Following the plan above, stitch or

crochet the motifs together as shown on page 26. First join seven motifs together to form a strip, then repeat with the remaining motifs until you have nine strips measuring the same length.
3 Join the strips together in the same way to make the completed bedspread. Press on the wrong side using a warm iron.

BUTTERFLY TABLECLOTH

Worked in filet crochet using fine cotton yarn, this delightful tablecloth features butterfly and rose motifs set within a deep zigzag border. Suitable for the experienced needlewoman, the border will take some time to complete, but the finished tablecloth will give you pleasure for years to come. When not in use, store the tablecloth wrapped in acid-free tissue paper in a cool, dry place.

Materials
White fine crochet cotton, No 40
White cotton or linen fabric
Steel crochet hook 0.6 mm
White sewing thread
Sewing needle
Pins

Measurements
Work sufficient pattern repeats to make a border to fit your table. When buying the fabric, remember to allow a hem allowance of 1.5 cm (⅝ in) all round.

Abbreviations
A full list of crochet abbreviations is given on page 22.
  Special abbreviations for this pattern:
sp(s) = space(s) = two chain, miss two chain or two treble, one treble into next chain or treble
blk(s) = block(s) = four treble (plus three treble for each additional block in group)
  More details of filet crochet are given on page 21.

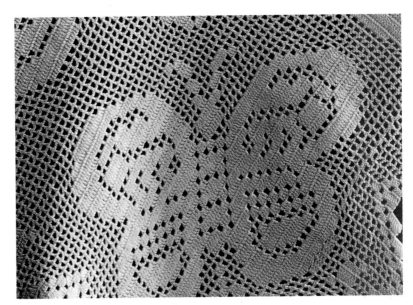

Working the border
FOUNDATION CHAIN Make 150ch.

ROW 1 1tr into 4th ch from hook, 5tr, 1sp, 3tr, 8sps, 18tr, 2sps, 9tr, 1sp, 6tr, 4sps, 3tr, 17sps, 3tr, turn.

ROW 2 3ch (stands as first tr), 3tr, 16sps, 1blk, 5sps, 5blks, 2sps, 1blk, 4sps, 2blks, 9sps, 1blk, 1sp, 1blk, turn.

Follow chart from third row (arrow on chart shows direction).
When decreasing at the beginning of a row, ss along the top of the blks and when making extension blks at the beginning of a row turn with 8ch; work 1tr into 4th ch from hook and 1tr into each rem ch.
Repeat the 48 pattern rows until the corner is reached, then work only until row 36. Continue straight, turning inside heavy line to top.
Fasten off.
Rejoin yarn at corner arrow.
Work 24 rows along row-ends.

ROW 25 Work across short row then continue along heavy line to inner corner. Continue from chart.

■ block

□ space

Butterflies dance amidst little rose motifs on this deep border worked in filet crochet using fine cotton yarn. The design is a satisfying task for the experienced needlewoman.

After last corner work 14 full width rows.
Fasten off.
Join inner edge of short rows to main border.
Join first and last border rows.

Making up the tablecloth
1 Sew in the ends. Pin out the border a section at a time following the illustrated instructions given on page 26. Spray with water and allow to dry completely before removing the pins.

2 Pin the border on to the fabric to check the fit and carefully cut away any surplus, remembering to leave a 1.5 cm (⅝ in) hem allowance round the edge. Remove the pins and turn a narrow double hem round the cloth and machine stitch or hem neatly by hand. Press the hem well.
3 Pin the border round the cloth, taking care to keep the points evenly spaced along each side. Using small, neat stitches, oversew the crochet border to the fabric. Press lightly on the wrong side with a warm iron.

HEARTS AND DIAMONDS BEDSPREAD

The bedspread is worked in long, narrow strips which are then crocheted together before a narrow border is worked. Make the bedspread in thick, double knitting weight cotton, either in the traditional white, or in a plain colour which coordinates with your bedroom furnishings. Alternatively, use up any oddments of yarn you have and work each strip in a different colour, working the joining stitches and border in either black of white yarn. If you do this, make sure that all the yarns you use are of identical thickness and fibre composition.

Materials
White double knitting weight
    cotton yarn
3.5 mm crochet hook
Tapestry needle size 22 or 24

Measurements
The bedspread is worked in long strips which are about 8 cm (3¼ in) wide. Make sufficient strips to fit the size of your bed, then join the strips together as shown below before working the edging.

Abbreviations
A full list of crochet abbreviations is given on page 22.

Special abbreviations for this pattern: pct (picot) = three chain, slip stitch in first of these three chain.

A challenging but quite stunning design, this lacy hearts and diamonds pattern is worked in long strips before being crocheted together.

Working the strips
First strip:
Work 27ch.

FOUNDATION ROW Into 4th ch from hook, work 3tr, 2ch, 4tr, 19ch, miss 22ch, [4tr, 2ch, 4tr] into last ch (1 shell made), turn.

ROW 1 (WRONG SIDE) 2ch, shell into first 2ch sp, 19ch, shell into 2ch sp, turn.

ROW 2 Rep row 1.

ROW 3 2ch, shell into first 2ch sp, 9ch, inserting hook under 4 loops work 1dc around the 4 loops together, turn, 3ch (counts as 1tr), 6tr into 9ch sp, turn, * 3ch, 1tr into each of next 6tr, turn; rep from * twice more, 3ch, shell into next 2ch sp, turn.

ROWS 4 TO 7 Rep row 1.

ROW 8 2 ch, shell into first 2ch sp, 9ch, inserting hook under 4 loops insert hook into top of diamond made and work 1dc with 4 loops together, turn, complete diamond as in row 3, 3ch, shell into next 2ch sp, turn.

ROWS 9 TO 12 Rep row 1.

ROW 13 Rep row 8.

Rep from row 4 for the pattern until the strip is the required length, ending with either a 7th or 12th pattern row.

NEXT ROW 2ch, shell into first 2ch sp, 9ch, work 1dc into top of diamond and around 4 loops together, 9ch, shell into next 2ch sp.

Fasten off. Work the remaining strips in the same way.

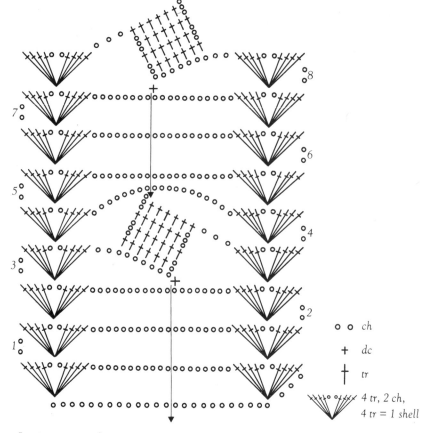

ch ○○
dc +
tr †
4 tr, 2 ch, 4 tr = 1 shell

Joining the strips
With the right side of the work facing, join the yarn in first 2ch turning sp on left-hand strip and work 1dc into this sp, * 4ch, 1dc into next 2ch turning sp on right-hand strip; rep from * until strips are joined.
   Fasten off.
   Repeat to join the rest of strips together.

Working the border
With the right side of the work facing, join yarn in corner 2ch turning sp. Work evenly a border of [2ch, 1dc in edge, pct] along strip to second corner, across the join work 2ch, pct, 2ch, cont in this way ending with [2ch, 1dc in edge, pct] across the last strip to corner, ending 1dc in corner.
   Fasten off.

Finishing off the bedspread
Sew in the ends. Press lightly on the wrong side with a warm iron.

SNOWFLAKE TRAYCLOTH

These quick-to-crochet snowflake motifs are joined together as you work, so the design requires no extra sewing except for finishing off the thread ends on the back. Make the traycloth the right size to fit your tray, then finish off the cloth with a simple two-row edging. By using a heavier white yarn, perhaps double knitting weight cotton, and working more snowflakes this design could also make a lovely, lacy bedspread to decorate a country-style bedroom.

Materials
White fine crochet cotton
2 mm crochet hook
Sewing needle
Pins
Starch (optional)

Measurements
Each motif measures approximately 9 cm (3½ in) across. Work sufficient motifs to cover the base of your tray, joining them together as you work, then work the edging round the outside.

Abbreviations
A full list of crochet abbreviations is given on page 22.

Working the motifs

FIRST SNOWFLAKE
Work 7ch and join with ss to form a ring.

ROUND 1 3ch (counts as 1tr), * 2ch, 1tr into ring; rep from * 10 times more, 2ch, join with ss into 3rd of 3ch. (12 spaced tr).

ROUND 2 3ch (counts as 1tr), * 3ch, 1tr in next tr; rep from * 10 times more, 3ch, join with ss into 3rd of 3ch. (12 spaced tr).

ROUND 3 * Into next loop work 1dc, 1htr, 1tr, 1htr, 1dc (1 shell made); rep from * 11 times more, join with ss into first dc. (12 shells).

ROUND 4 Ss across next htr and into tr at top of shell, * 7 ch, 1dc into tr at centre of next shell; rep from * 10 times more, 7 ch, join with ss into first of 7 ch.

●	ss
o	ch
+	dc
†	htr
†	tr
■	joining place
⊗	picot

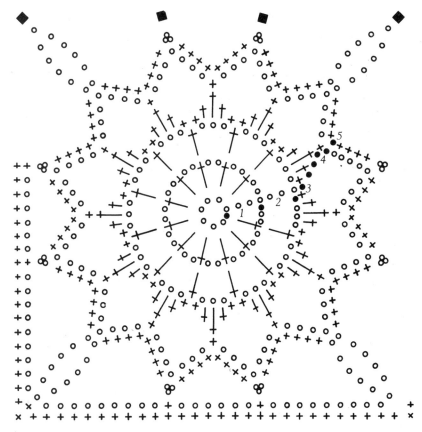

ROUND 5 * Into next loop work 4dc, 11ch, 4dc to form corner, into each of next 2 loops work 4dc, 3ch to form picot, 4dc; rep from * 3 times more, join with ss into first dc.

Fasten off.

SECOND SNOWFLAKE

Work as given above for the first motif until round 4 has been completed, then join second motif to first motif as follows:

ROUND 5 Into first loop of second motif work 4dc, 5ch, place WS of both motifs together and join by working 1dc into 11ch corner loop of first motif, 5ch, return to first loop of second motif, work another 4dc to complete corner, * into next loop work 4dc, 1ch, 1dc into matching picot of first motif, 1ch, 4dc into same loop of second motif, rep from * once more, then into next corner loop of second motif work 4dc, 5ch, 1dc into 11ch corner loop of first motif, 5ch, another 4dc into same loop of second motif to complete corner, work remainder of motif as given for first motif.

Work all further snowflake motifs as given for the second motif, joining the motifs together in the same way as you work. Take care that corner loops are joined with 1dc on the right side whether there are two, three or four corners meeting.

Working the edging
Rejoin the yarn in the first 3ch sp on long edge.

ROW 1 1dc in same sp, * 6ch, 1dc in next 3ch sp, 9ch, 1dc where 11ch loops meet, 9ch; rep from * to end, working

[9ch, 1dc into 11ch loop, 9ch] into single 11ch loop at each corner, join with ss to first dc.

ROW 2 1ch, * 6dc into 6ch loop, 1dc into next dc, 9dc into 9ch loop, 1dc into next dc; rep from * to end, working 3dc

This charming traycloth is crocheted speedily using an attractive snowflake motif. No additional sewing is needed as the motifs are joined together as you work.

into dc at each corner, join with ss into first ch.
Fasten off.

Finishing the traycloth
1 Sew in the ends. Pin out the cloth round the border following the illustrated in- structions given on page 26. Spray with water and allow to dry thoroughly before removing the pins.
2 For a stiffer finish, starch the cloth before pinning it out and finish off by pressing lightly on the wrong side using a warm iron.

SCALLOPED SHELF EDGINGS

These two scalloped edgings are quickly crocheted in thick cotton yarn and they are the perfect way of adding decoration to kitchen or bathroom shelves holding pretty china. Both edgings are worked widthways, so it is easy to make a strip which is just the right length for your shelf. Remember to finish the edging at the end of one complete repeat so that both ends of the strip will match.

White is the classic colour for this type of decoration, but you could work the designs using deep or pastel shades of yarn if you prefer. Attach the edgings to the shelves with sticky fixing pads so they can be removed easily for laundering.

Materials
White medium-weight No 3 mercerized cotton yarn
3.50 mm crochet hook
Pins

Measurements
Each edging measures approximately 12 cm (4¾ in) deep across the widest point. Each repeat worked will make about 5 cm (2 in) of edging.

Abbreviations
Crochet abbreviations appear on page 22. Special abbreviations for this pattern:
1p = loop

Working the top edging
Work 27ch.

FOUNDATION ROW 1tr into 4th ch from hook, 1tr into each of next 2ch, 2ch, miss 2ch, 1tr into each of next 10ch, 2ch, miss 2ch, 1tr into each of next 7ch, turn.

ROW 1 9ch, ss into 2nd ch from hook and into each of next 3ch, 1tr into each of 8th and 9th ch from hook, (this counts as 3 spare ch for next row, plus 3tr), 1tr into each of next 7tr, 2ch, 1tr into next tr, [2ch, miss 2tr, 1tr into next tr] 3 times, 2ch, 1tr into next tr, 1tr into each of next 2tr, 1tr into top of 3ch, turn.

ROW 2 3ch (counts as first tr), miss 1tr, 1tr into each of next 3tr, [2ch, 1tr into next tr] twice, 2tr into 2ch sp, 1tr into next tr, [2ch, 1tr into next tr] twice, 1tr into each of next 6tr, 2ch, miss 2tr, 1tr into next tr, 1tr into each of the 3 spare ch made on the previous row, turn.

ROW 3 5ch, 1tr into 4th ch from hook, 1tr into next ch, 1tr into next tr, 2ch, miss 2tr, 1tr into next tr, 2tr into next 2ch sp, 1tr into next tr, 2ch, miss 2tr, 1tr into each of next 4tr, 2ch, 1tr into next tr, 2tr into 2ch sp, 1tr into next tr, 2ch, miss 2tr, 1tr into next tr, 2tr into 2ch sp, 1tr into next tr, 2ch, 1tr into each of next 3tr, 1tr in top of 3ch, turn.

ROW 4 3ch, 1tr into each of next 3tr, 2ch, 1tr into next tr, 2ch, miss 2tr, 1tr into next tr, 2tr into 2ch sp, 1tr into next tr, 2ch, miss 2tr, 1tr into next tr, 2ch, 1tr into each of next 4tr, 2tr into 2ch sp, 1tr into next tr, 2ch, miss 2tr, 1tr into next tr, 2tr into 2ch sp, 1tr into next tr, turn.

ROW 5 Ss over first 4tr, 3ch (counts as first tr), 2tr into 2ch sp, 1tr into each of next 7tr, [2ch, 1tr into next tr] twice,

A lovely old-fashioned idea which has recently been revived are these decorative shelf edgings. For those with a little more than basic skills, they make a quick and rewarding project.

2ch, miss 2tr, 1tr into next tr, [2ch, 1tr into next tr] twice, 1tr into each of next 2tr, 1tr in top of 3ch, turn.

ROW 6 3ch, 1tr into each of next 3tr, 2ch, 1tr into next tr, [2tr into 2ch sp, 1tr into next tr] 3 times, 2ch, 1tr into next tr, 1tr into each of next 6tr, turn.

Repeat rows 1 to 6 until the edging is the required length, ending with a 6th row.
Fasten off.

Bottom edging
Work 27ch.

FOUNDATION ROW 1tr into 4th ch from hook, 1tr into each of next 2ch [2ch, miss 2ch, 1tr into each of next 4ch] twice, 2ch, miss 2ch, 1tr into each of next 7ch, turn.

ROW 1 9ch, ss into 2nd ch from hook and into each of next 3ch, 1tr into each of 8th and 9th ch from hook, (this counts as 3 spare ch for next row, plus 3tr), 1tr into each of next 4tr, [2ch, miss 2tr, 1tr into next tr, 2tr into 2ch lp, 1tr into next tr] 3 times, 1tr into each of next 3tr, 1tr into top of 3ch, turn.

ROW 2 3ch (counts as first tr), 1tr into each of next 3tr, [2ch, miss 2tr, 1tr into next tr, 2tr into 2ch lp, 1tr into next tr] twice, 2ch, miss 2tr, 1tr into each of next 4tr, 1tr into each of the 3 spare ch made on the previous row, turn.

ROW 3 5ch, 1tr into 4th ch from hook, 1tr into next ch, 1tr into each of next 4tr, [2ch, miss 2tr, 1tr into next tr, 2tr into 2ch lp, 1tr into next tr] 3 times, 2ch, miss 2tr, 1tr into next tr, 2tr into next 2ch sp, 1tr into each of next 3tr, 1tr into top of 3ch, turn.

ROW 4 3ch (counts as first tr), 1tr into each of next 3tr, [2ch, miss 2tr, 1tr into next tr, 2tr into 2ch lp, 1tr into next tr] 3 times, 2ch, miss 2tr, 1tr into next tr, 2tr into 2ch sp, 1tr into each of next 4tr, turn.

ROW 5 Ss over first 4tr, 3ch (counts as first tr), 1tr into each of next 2tr, 2tr into 2ch sp, 1tr into next tr, [2ch, miss 2tr, 1tr into next tr, 2tr into 2ch lp, 1tr into next tr] 3 times, 1tr into each of next 2tr, 1tr in top of 3ch, turn.

ROW 6 3ch, 1tr into each of next 3tr, [2ch, miss 2tr, 1tr into each of next 4tr] twice, 2ch, miss 2tr, 1tr into each of next 7tr, turn.

Repeat rows 1 to 6 until edging is the required length, ending with a 6th row.
Fasten off.

Finishing the edgings
Pin out each edging in sections following instructions on page 26. Spray with water and allow each section to dry completely before moving on to the next one.

● ss

○ ch

† tr

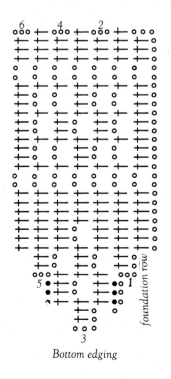

Bottom edging

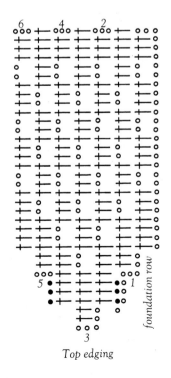

Top edging

ROSES
PINCUSHIONS

Two filet crochet rose designs make a pair of useful and ornamental pincushions to keep your pins and needles safe. Backed with white felt and decorated with cotton lace and ribbon trims, either design would make a lovely present for a friend. To make a personalized pincushion, substitute the rose with initials from the alphabet on page 77, centring the letters in a filet crochet rectangle.

Materials (for both designs)

Cream fine crochet cotton
White felt
1.25 mm crochet hook
White ready-frilled cotton lace edging
Cream ready-made ribbon roses
Cream stranded embroidery cotton
Polyester toy stuffing
Tacking cotton
Crewel embroidery needle
Sewing needle
Pins

Measurements

The smaller pincushion measures 11 cm × 12.5 cm (4¼ in × 5 in) minus the edging and the larger one measures 12.5 cm × 15 cm (5 in × 6 in).

Abbreviations

A full list of crochet abbreviations is given on page 22.
Special abbreviations for this pattern:
sp(s) = space(s) (2ch, miss 2ch or 2tr, 1tr into next ch or tr)
blk(s) = block(s) (4tr, plus 3tr for each additional block in group)

More details of how to work filet crochet are given on page 21.

Large pincushion

FOUNDATION CHAIN Make 60 ch.

ROW 1 1tr into 4th ch from hook, 1tr into each ch across row.
(58tr)

ROW 2 3ch (counts as 1tr), 1tr into next 3tr, 6sps, 2blks, 9sps, 1blk, turn.
Follow the chart from the third row until the complete design has been worked.
Fasten off.

Small pincushion

FOUNDATION CHAIN Make 52ch.
ROW 1 1tr into 4th ch from hook, 1tr into each ch across row.

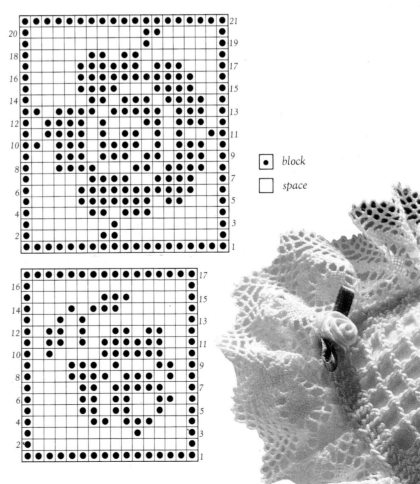

● block
□ space

ROW 2 3ch (counts as 1tr), 1tr into next 3tr, 14sps, 1blk, turn.

Follow the chart from the third row until the design is complete.
Fasten off.

Making up the pincushions
Both designs are made up as follows:
1 Sew in the ends. Pin out the rose motif following the illustrated instructions given on page 26. Spray with water and allow the crochet to dry completely before removing the pins.
2 Pin the crochet on to the felt and cut round the edge leaving a margin of at least 2.5 cm (1 in) all round. Cut out a second piece of felt to the same size. Tack the lace edging to the wrong side of the crochet, neatly turning under the raw ends.
3 Place the backing felt on a flat surface. Cover with the other piece, then place the lace-trimmed crochet right side upwards on top. Tack all the layers together.
4 Using three strands of embroidery thread and beginning at the centre of one of the long sides, stitch through the layers close to the edge of the crochet. Use double running stitch and make sure you catch the lace edging with the stitching. Leave an opening of about 5 cm (2 in) along the last side and do not break off the thread.
5 Remove the tacking stitches which are holding the layers together, but not those securing the lace edging. Stuff the pincushion carefully with polyester stuffing, using the point of the crochet hook to help you gently manoeuvre the stuffing right into the corners.
6 Using the attached thread, complete the outside row of stitching and fasten off securely. Remove the tacking stitches from the lace. Turn the pincushion over and carefully trim away the surplus felt round the edge. Sew a ribbon rose in each corner of the crocheted square design.

Pretty little pincushions display two quick-to-work rose motifs. Decorated with little ribbon roses and lace edging, they make ideal gifts.

CROCHET BAGS

Crochet bags are fun to work and they are useful in many ways around the home. The two bags shown here hold soap and bathroom accessories and could be hung on the back of the door or looped on to a towel rail. Worked in other colours of yarn, the bags would be perfect for daytime or evening wear, accommodating purse, keys, handkerchief, makeup bag – and even a paperback novel – with ease, while the same bag worked in sturdy string would be useful for carrying shopping home.

Materials
Cream double knitting weight cotton or ribbon yarn
3.5 mm crochet hook
Tapestry needle

Measurements
Each bag measures approximately 19 cm (7½ in) round the widest part and 28 cm (11 in) from top to the centre of the base.

Abbreviations
A full list of crochet abbreviations is given on page 22.

COTTON YARN BAG

Working the bag
Work 6ch and join with ss to form a ring.

ROUND 1 5ch, * 2tr into ring, 2ch, rep from * 4 times more, 1tr into ring, ss to 3rd of first 5ch.

ROUND 2 Ss into 2ch sp, 5ch, 1tr into same sp, * 1tr into each of next 2tr, [1tr, 2ch, 1tr] into 2ch sp; rep from * 4 times more, 1tr into each of next 2tr, ss to 3rd of 5ch.

ROUND 3 Ss into 2ch sp, 5ch, 1tr into same sp, * 1tr into each of next 4tr, [1tr, 2ch, 1tr] into 2ch sp; rep from * 4 times more, 1tr into each of next 4tr, ss to 3rd of first 5ch.

ROUNDS 4 AND 5 Work 2 more rounds in the same way, working 2 more tr along each side each time.

ROUND 6 Ss into 2ch sp, 5ch, * miss 1tr, 1tr into each of next 8tr, 2ch, 1tr into 2ch sp, 2ch; rep from * to end, but omit last 1tr and 2ch and ss to 3rd of 5ch.

ROUND 7 Ss into 2ch sp, 5ch, * work tr2tog, 1tr into each of next 4tr, tr2tog, 2ch, [1tr into 2ch sp, 2ch] twice; rep from * 5 times more, but omit last 1tr and 2ch and ss to 3rd of first 5ch.

ROUND 8 Ss into 2ch sp, 5ch, * work tr2tog, 1tr into each of next 2tr, tr2tog, 2ch, 1tr into 2ch sp, 2ch, 3tr into 2ch sp, 2ch, 1tr into 2ch sp, 2ch; rep from * 5 times more but omit last tr and 2ch and ss to 3rd of first 5ch.

ROUND 9 Ss over 2ch sp and into next tr, 3ch, 1tr into each of next 3tr, * 2ch, miss next 2ch sp, 1tr into next 2ch sp, 1tr into each of next 3tr, 1tr into next 2ch sp, miss next 2ch sp, 1tr into each of next 4tr; rep from * 5 times more but omit last 4tr and ss to 3rd of first 3ch.

ROUND 10 Ss into next tr, 3ch, 1tr into next tr, * 2ch, 1tr into 2ch sp, 1tr into each of next 5tr, 1tr into 2ch sp, 2ch, miss 1tr, 1tr into each of next 2tr; rep

The basic pattern for these lovely little bags can easily be adjusted to make other types: an evening purse perhaps or even a shopping holdall.

from * 5 times more but omit last 2tr and ss to 3rd of first 3ch.

ROUND 11 3ch, 1tr into next tr, * 3tr into 2ch sp, 1tr into each of next 7tr, 3tr into 2ch sp, 1tr into each of next 2tr; rep from * 5 times more but omit last 2tr and ss to 3rd of first 3ch. (90tr)

ROUND 12 3ch, tr2tog, * 3 ch, tr3tog; rep from * 28 times more, 3ch, ss to top of first group of tr.

ROUND 13 Ss to centre of 3ch sp, 4ch, * 1dc into next 3ch sp, 3ch; rep from * to end, ss to first of first 4ch.

ROUND 14 Ss to centre of first 3ch sp, 3ch, 2tr into same sp, 3tr into each 3ch sp all round, ss into 3rd of first 3ch. (90tr)

ROUND 15 4ch, * miss next tr, 1tr into next tr, 1ch; rep from * to end, ss into 3rd of first 4ch.

ROUND 16 Ss into 1ch sp, 4ch, * 1tr into next 1ch sp, 1ch; rep from * to end, ss to 3rd of first 4ch.

ROUNDS 17, 18 AND 19 Rep round 16 3 times more.

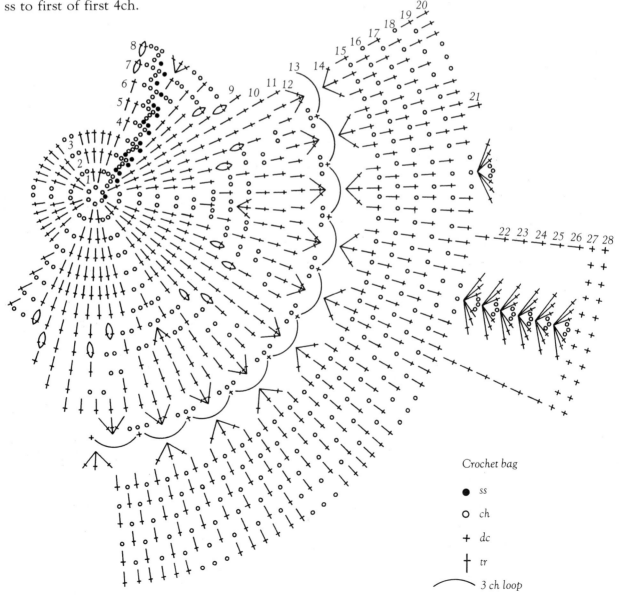

Crochet bag

● ss

○ ch

+ dc

✝ tr

⌒ 3 ch loop

ROUND 20 3ch, [1tr into 1ch sp, 1tr into next tr] twice, 1tr into 1ch sp, * 3ch, miss 3sts, 1tr into each of next 6 sts; rep from * 8 times more, 3ch, miss 3 sts, ss to 3rd of first 3ch.

ROUND 21 Ss over next 2tr, 3ch, * [3tr, 3ch, 3tr] into 3ch sp, 1tr between 3rd and 4th tr of 6tr; rep from * 8 times more, [3tr, 3ch, 3tr] into 3ch sp, ss to 3rd of first 3ch.

ROUND 22 3ch, * [3tr, 3ch, 3tr] into 3ch sp, 1tr into single tr; rep from * 8 times more, [3tr, 3ch, 3tr] into 3ch sp, ss to 3rd of first 3ch.

ROUNDS 23, 24, 25 AND 26 Rep round 22 4 times more.

ROUND 27 1ch, 1dc into next 3tr, * 3dc into 3ch sp, 1dc into next 7tr; rep from * to end, ss into first dc.

ROUND 28 1ch, 1dc into each dc on previous round, ss into first dc. Fasten off.

RIBBON YARN BAG
Work 6ch and join with a ss to form a ring.

ROUND 1 5ch, * 2tr into ring, 2ch; rep from * 4 times more, 1tr into ring, ss to 3rd of first 5ch.

ROUND 2 Ss into 2ch sp, 5ch, 1tr into same sp, * 1tr into each of next 2tr, [1tr, 2ch, 1tr] into 2ch sp; rep from * 4 times more, 1tr into each of next 2tr, ss to 3rd of 5ch.

ROUND 3 Ss into 2ch sp, 5ch, 1tr into same sp, * 1tr into each of next 4tr, [1tr, 2ch, 1tr] into 2ch sp; rep from * 4 times more, 1tr into each of next 4tr, ss to 3rd of first 5ch.

ROUNDS 4 AND 5 Work 2 more rounds in the same way, working 2 more tr along each side each time.

ROUND 6 Ss into 2ch sp, 5ch, * miss 1tr, 1tr into each of next 8tr, 2ch, 1tr into 2ch sp, 2ch; rep from * to end, but omit last 1tr and 2ch and ss to 3rd of 5ch.

ROUND 7 Ss into 2ch sp, 5ch, * work tr2tog, 1tr into each of next 4tr, tr2tog, 2ch, [1tr into 2ch sp, 2ch] twice; rep

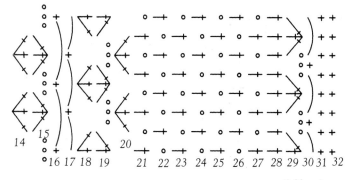

Ribbon bag

1st to 14th rows alike for both bags

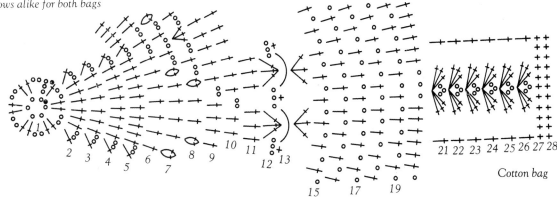

Cotton bag

from * 5 times more, but omit last 1tr and 2ch and ss to 3rd of first 5ch.

ROUND 8 Ss into 2ch sp, 5ch, * work tr2tog, 1tr into each of next 2tr, tr2tog, 2ch, 1tr into 2ch sp, 2ch, 3tr into 2ch sp, 2ch, 1tr into 2ch sp, 2ch; rep from * 5 times more but omit last tr and 2ch and ss to 3rd of first 5ch.

ROUND 9 Ss over 2ch sp and into next tr, 3ch, 1tr into each of next 3tr, * 2ch, miss next 2ch sp, 1tr into next 2ch sp, 1tr into each of next 3tr, 1tr into next 2ch sp, miss next 2ch sp, 1tr into each of next 4tr; rep from * 5 times more but omit last 4tr and ss to 3rd of first 3ch.

ROUND 10 Ss into next tr, 3ch, 1tr into next tr, * 2ch, 1tr into 2ch sp, 1tr into each of next 5tr, 1tr into 2ch sp, 2ch, miss 1tr, 1tr into each of next 2tr; rep from * 5 times more but omit last 2tr and ss to 3rd of first 3ch.

ROUND 11 3ch, 1tr into next tr, * 3tr into 2ch sp, 1tr into each of next 7tr, 3tr into 2ch sp, 1tr into each of next 2tr; rep from * 5 times more but omit last 2tr and ss to 3rd of first 3ch. (90tr)

ROUND 12 3ch, work tr2tog, * 3ch, tr3tog; rep from * 28 times more, 3ch, ss to top of first group of tr.

ROUND 13 Ss to centre of 3ch sp, 4ch, * 1dc into next 3ch sp, 3ch; rep from * to end, ss to first of first 4ch.

ROUND 14 Ss to centre of first 3ch sp, 3ch, 2tr into same sp, 3tr into each 3ch sp all round, ss to 3rd of first 3ch. (90tr)

ROUNDS 15 AND 18 Rep round 12.

ROUNDS 16 AND 19 Rep round 13.

ROUNDS 17 AND 20 Rep round 14.

ROUND 21 4ch, * miss next tr, 1tr into next tr, 1ch; rep from * to end, ss to 3rd of first 4ch.

ROUND 22 Ss into 1ch sp, 4ch, * 1tr into next 1ch sp, 1ch; rep from * to end, ss to 3rd of first 4ch.

ROUNDS 23, 24, 25, 26 AND 27 Rep round 22.

ROUND 28 3ch, 1tr into next ch sp, * 1tr into next tr, 1tr into ch sp; rep from * to end, ss to 3rd of 3ch. (90tr)

ROUND 29 Rep round 12.

ROUND 30 Rep round 13.

ROUND 31 Ss into next 3ch sp, 1ch, 2dc into first 3ch sp, * 3dc into next 3ch sp; rep from * to end, ss to ch.

ROUND 32 1ch, 1dc into each dc on previous round, ss into first dc. Fasten off.

Making the cords
Cut 12 lengths of yarn, each 120 cm (47 in) long. Plait 6 lengths for each cord, knotting the ends to leave a group of threads about 8 cm (3 in) long at each end.

Making up the bags
Sew in the ends. Press cotton yarn lightly on the wrong side if necessary, but do not press ribbon yarn. Thread one cord through the row of holes along the top of the bag then thread the second cord through the same holes so the loose ends emerge on the opposite side of the bag. Knot each pair of loose ends together about 1 cm (½ in) above the existing knots.

LAVENDER BAGS

Delicate crochet hexagons worked in fine white cotton are backed with a contrasting colour felt to make a pair of delightful lavender bags. Felt does not fray in use, so a decorative edge is quickly made by cutting the felt margin round the crochet with a pair of pinking shears.

Materials
White fine cotton yarn
Contrasting felt
1.25 mm crochet hook
Stranded cotton to match felt
Crewel embroidery needle
Sewing needle
Tacking thread
Pins
Dried lavender

Measurements
Each sachet measures about 12 cm (4¾ in).

Dried lavender has been used for centuries, not only to keep stored linen and lingerie sweet-smelling, but also to ward off moths. Fill these simple-to-crochet sachets with a handful as a gift or for your own use.

Abbreviations
A full list of crochet abbreviations is given on page 22.

WINDMILL HEXAGON
Work 5ch and join with ss to form a ring.
ROUND 1 * 6ch, 1dc into ring; rep from * 5 times more, ss over first 3ch of first 6ch lp.

ROUND 2 * 4ch, 1dc into 6ch lp; rep from * 5 times more, working last dc into ss before 4 ch.

ROUND 3 * 4ch, 2dc into 4ch lp, 1dc into dc; rep from * 5 times more, working last dc into last dc at end of round 2.

ROUND 4 * 4ch, 2dc into 4ch lp, 1dc into each of next 2dc; rep from * to end.

ROUND 5 * 4ch, 2dc into 4ch lp, 1dc into each of next 3dc; rep from * to end.

Cont in this way, working 1 more dc in each group on each round until there are 9dc in each group.

ROUND 10 * 4ch, 2tr into 4ch lp, 1tr into each of next 8dc; rep from * to end.

ROUND 11 * 4ch, 2tr into 4ch lp, 1tr into each of next 9tr; rep from * to end.

ROUND 12 Ss into first ch of 4ch lp, 1ch, * [2dc, 3ch, 2dc] into 4ch lp, 1dc into each tr along side; rep from * to end, join with ss into 1ch.

ROUND 13 3ch, 1tr into next dc, * [2tr, 3ch, 2tr] into 3ch sp, 1tr into each tr along side; rep from * to end, ss into 3rd of 3ch.

ROUND 14 1ch, 1dc into next tr, * 5dc into 3ch sp, 1dc into each tr along side; rep from * to end, ss into 1ch.
Fasten off.

FLOWER HEXAGON
Work 6ch. Join with ss to form ring.
ROUND 1 4ch, [1tr into ring, 1ch] 11 times, join with ss to 3rd of 4ch.

ROUND 2 3ch, 2tr into sp, 1tr into tr, 2ch, * 1tr into tr, 2tr into sp, 1tr into tr, 2ch; rep from * 4 times more, join with ss to 3rd of 3ch.

ROUND 3 3ch, 1tr into same place, 1tr into each of next 2tr, 2tr into next tr, 2ch, * 2tr into next tr, 1tr into each of next 2tr, 2tr into next tr, 2ch; rep from * 4 times, join with ss to 3rd of 3ch.

ROUND 4 3ch, 1tr into same place, 1tr into each of next 4tr, 2tr into next tr, 2ch, * 2 tr into next tr, 1tr into each of next 4tr, 2tr into next tr, 2ch; rep from * 4 times, join with ss to 3rd of 3ch.

ROUND 5 3ch, 1tr into each of next 7tr, * 3ch, 1dc into 2ch sp, 3ch, 1tr into each of next 8tr; rep from * 4 times more, 3ch, 1dc into 2ch sp, 3ch, join with ss to 3rd of 3ch.

ROUND 6 Ss into next tr, 3ch, 1tr into each of next 5tr, * 3ch, [1dc into 3ch sp, 3ch] twice, miss next tr, 1 tr into each of next 6tr; rep from * 4 times more, 3ch, [1dc into 3ch sp, 3ch] twice, join with ss to 3rd of 3ch.

ROUND 7 Ss into next tr, 3ch, 1tr into each of next 3tr, * 3ch, [1dc into 3ch sp, 3ch] 3 times, miss next tr, 1tr into each of next 4tr; rep from * 4 times more, 3ch, [1dc into 3ch sp, 3ch] 3 times, join with ss to 3rd of 3ch.

ROUND 8 Ss between 2nd and 3rd tr of group, 3ch, 1tr into same place, * 3ch, [1dc into 3ch sp, 3ch] 4 times, 2tr between 2nd and 3rd tr of group; rep from * 4 times more, 3ch, [1dc into 3ch sp, 3ch] 4 times, join with ss to 3rd of 3ch.

ROUND 9 Ss into 3ch sp, 3ch, 3tr into same sp, [4tr into 3ch sp] 4 times, * 3ch, miss 2tr, [4tr into 3ch sp] 5 times; rep from * 4 times more, 3 ch, join with ss to 3rd of 3ch.

ROUND 10 1ch, * 1dc into each tr along edge, 5dc into 3ch sp; rep from * 5 times more, join with ss to first ch. Fasten off.

Making up the bags

1 Sew in the ends. Pin out the hexagon motif following the illustrated instructions given on page 26. Spray with water and allow to dry thoroughly before removing the pins.

2 Pin the motif on to the felt and cut round the edge leaving a margin of at least 2.5 cm (1 in) all round. Cut out a second piece of felt to the same size.

3 Place the backing felt on a flat surface. Cover with the other piece, then centre the crochet motif on top, right side up. Tack all the layers together.

4 Using three strands of embroidery thread and beginning about 1 cm (½ in) to the right of the first corner, stitch through all the layers close to the edge of the crochet using double running stitch. Leave an opening of about 2.5 cm (1 in) along the last side and do not break off the thread.

5 Remove the tacking and fill the bag with dried lavender. Using the attached thread, close up the opening and fasten off the edges securely.

6 Finally trim away the surplus felt about 6 mm (¼ in) from the edge of the crochet using pinking shears.

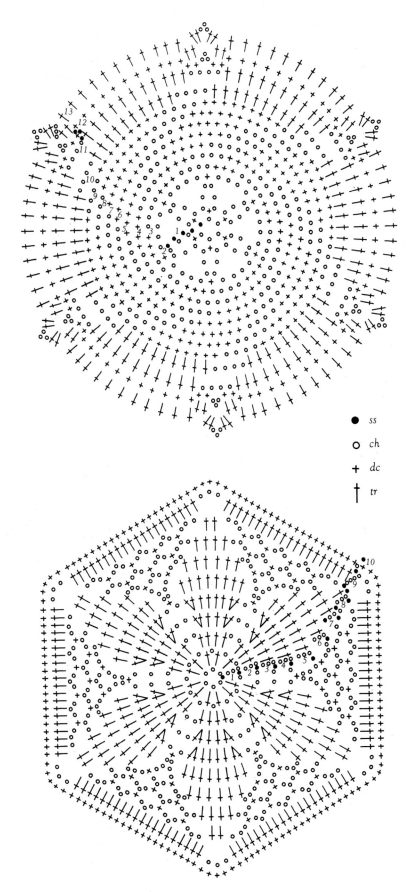

●   ss

○   ch

+   dc

†   tr

CHRISTMAS STARS

Tiny, five-pointed crochet stars make such pretty Christmas tree decorations. Work the pattern in fine cotton, then dip the stars into a solution of stiff-finish starch or PVA craft medium (white craft glue) diluted with cold water. Make sure you let each star dry thoroughly after pinning it out to shape, then remove the pins, thread narrow ribbon through one of the points and hang the star on the tree. You could also work this design in fine gold or silver yarn.

Materials
White crochet cotton size 10
1 mm crochet hook
Red narrow satin ribbon
Stiff-finish starch or PVA craft medium
Tapestry needle size 22 or 24
Pins

Measurements
Each star measures approximately 9 cm (3½ in) across. You can make larger stars by working the same pattern using a thicker yarn and larger hook.

Abbreviations
A full list of crochet abbreviations is given on page 22.

Working the stars
Centre (make 1):
Work 5ch and join with ss to form a ring.

ROUND 1 3ch, 1tr into ring, [2ch, 2tr into ring] 4 times more, 2ch, ss to 3rd of 3ch.

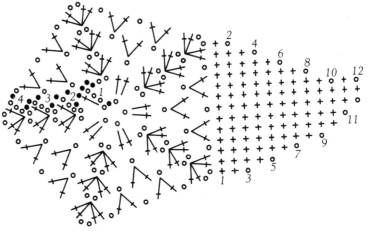

The perfect project for a beginner, these delightful little stars look wonderful against the deep green foliage of the traditional Christmas tree. If you only want to make a few, try working them in gold or silver yarn to highlight your tree.

ROUND 4 Ss into next 2ch sp, work beg shell into same sp, [1ch, 2tr into next 1ch sp] twice, 1ch, [shell into next 2ch sp, 1ch, 2tr into next 1ch sp, 1ch, 2tr into next 1ch sp, 1ch] 4 times, ss to 3rd of 3ch.
Fasten off.

Points (make 5):
ROW 1 Rejoin yarn in any 2ch space of shell, 1ch, 1dc into same sp, [1dc into each of next 2tr and ch sp] 4 times, 1ch, turn.
(13dc)

ROW 2 Miss first dc, work dc across row, 1ch, turn.
(12dc).

ROWS 3 TO 11 Rep row 2, missing first dc at beg of every row to decrease 1st.
(3dc rem at end of row 11)

ROW 12 1dc into 2nd dc, ss into next dc.
Fasten off.

To work subsequent star points, rejoin yarn in same 2ch sp where row 1 of previous point began and rep rows 1 to 12 to complete each point.

Finishing off the stars
1 Sew in the ends. Starch the stars stiffly following the manufacturer's instructions or dip each one into a solution of PVA (white craft glue) and water. Pin out the stars following the illustrated instructions given on page 26 and allow them to dry completely before removing the pins.
2 Thread a length of narrow red ribbon through the tip of one point on each star and tie it to form a hanging loop.

- ● ss
- ○ ch
- + dc
- † tr
- ⚓ 1 shell

ROUND 2 Ss into next 2ch sp, 3ch, 1tr into same space, 2ch, 2tr into same sp (beg shell made), 1ch, into next 2ch sp work 2tr, 2ch, 2tr (shell made), [1ch, 1 shell into next 2ch sp] 3 times more, 1ch, join with ss to 3rd of 3ch.

ROUND 3 Ss into next 2ch sp, work beg shell into same sp, 1ch, 2tr into next 1ch sp, 1ch, [shell into next 2ch sp, 1ch, 2tr into next 1ch sp, 1ch] 4 times, ss to 3rd of 3ch.

Pattern Library

CROCHET EDGINGS

Here are four different crochet edgings to try. Work the cream or green edging in fine cotton with a small hook – the finished effect will be narrow and delicate, perfect for lingerie. The peach and beige edgings are substantial enough to edge a traycloth or small tablecloth.

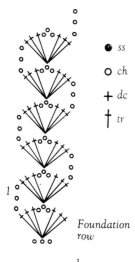

● ss
○ ch
+ dc
† tr

Foundation row

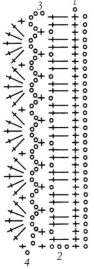

Abbreviations
Crochet abbreviations appear on page 22.

INTERWOVEN CROCHET BRAID (green)
Work 3ch.
FOUNDATION ROW Work * 3tr, 3ch, 3tr, 3ch, * into 2nd ch from hook, turn.
ROW 1 Rep from * to * into 3ch sp of previous row, turn.
Repeat row 1.

NARROW SHELLS (cream)
Work a multiple of 6ch plus 3.
FOUNDATION ROW Work 1dc into 2nd ch from hook, 1dc into each ch to end, turn.
ROW 1 3ch, miss first dc, 1tr into next dc, * 1ch, miss 1dc, 1tr into each of next 2dc; rep from * to end, turn.

ROW 2 5ch, 1dc into next ch sp, * 4ch, 1dc into next ch sp; rep from * to last 2 sts, 2ch, 1tr into 3rd of 3ch, turn.
ROW 3 1ch, 1dc into first tr, * 5tr into next 4ch sp, 1dc into next 4ch sp; rep from * to end, working last dc into 3rd of 5ch.

SCALLOPED EDGING (peach)

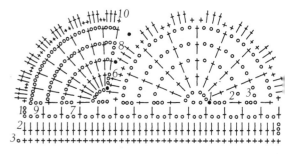

Work 8ch and join with ss; form ring.
ROW 1 3ch, 8tr into ring, turn.
ROW 2 4ch, 1tr into next tr, * 1ch, 1tr into next tr; rep from * 5 times more, 1ch, 1tr into 3rd of 3ch.
ROW 3 5ch, 1tr into next tr, * 2 ch, 1tr into next tr; rep from * 5 times more, 2ch, 1tr into 3rd of 4ch.
ROW 4 6ch, 1tr into next tr, * 3ch, 1tr into next tr; rep from * 5 times more, 3ch, 1tr into 3rd of 5ch.
ROW 5 * [1dc, 3tr, 1dc] into 3ch sp; rep from * 7 times more, 8ch, turn and ss into 2nd of first 3tr, turn.
ROW 6 3ch, 1tr into 8ch lp, turn.
ROW 7 4ch, 1tr into next tr, * 1ch, 1tr into next tr; rep from * 5 times more, 1ch, 1tr into 3rd of 3ch, ss into 2nd tr of next group of 3tr, turn.
ROW 8 5ch, miss first tr, 1tr into next tr; rep row 3 from * to end, turn.
ROW 9 Rep row 4, then ss into 2nd tr of next group of 3tr, turn.
Repeat rows 5 to 9, finishing with a 5th row, but omitting the 8ch at the end of the row.

Heading:

ROW 1 Working along top straight edge of scalloped edging, work 5ch, 1tr into next row-end, * 2ch, 1tr into next row-end; rep from * to end, turn.

ROW 2 3ch, * 2tr into 2ch sp, 1tr into next tr; rep from * to end, working last tr into 3rd of 5ch.

ROW 3 1ch, * 1dc into each tr; rep from * to end, working last dc into 3rd of 3ch. Fasten off.

EDWARDIAN FENCE EDGING *(beige)*

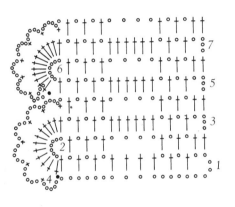

Work 20ch.

ROW 1 Work 1tr into 7th ch from hook, [1ch, miss 1ch, 1tr into next ch], twice, 2tr into each of next 2ch, [1tr into next ch, 1ch, miss 1ch] 3 times, 1tr into last st, 7ch, turn.

ROW 2 1tr into first 1ch sp, [1ch, 1tr into next 1ch sp] twice, 4ch, [1tr into next 1ch sp, 1ch] twice, 1tr into top of turning ch, 1tr into next ch, 4ch, turn.

ROW 3 [1tr into next 1ch sp, 1ch] twice, 6tr into 4ch lp, [1ch, 1tr into next 1ch sp] twice, 1ch, 12tr into 7ch lp at end of row and secure with a ss into last st of foundation ch, 5ch, turn.

ROW 4 1dc into 2nd st, [5ch, miss 1st, 1dc into next st] 5 times, 1ch, [1tr into next 1ch sp, 1ch] twice, 1tr into next 1ch sp, 4ch, [1tr into next 1ch sp, 1ch] twice, 1tr into first st of turning ch, 1tr into next st, 4ch, turn.

ROW 5 [1tr into next 1ch sp, 1ch] twice, 6tr into 4ch lp, 1ch, [1tr into next 1ch sp, 1ch] twice, 1tr into first of 5ch, 7ch, turn.

ROW 6 Rep row 2.

ROW 7 Rep row 3, but after working the 12tr group, work a ss into the st of 5ch close to the tr previously worked.

ROW 8 Rep row 4.

Repeat rows 5 to 8.

CROCHET BORDERS

The two deep crochet borders take their inspiration from traditional Irish crochet patterns. Suitable for edging a wide variety of household articles – from towels to pillowcases, either border can also be used as a shelf edging. For a more delicate result, try working the border designs in a fine mercerized crochet cotton using a small hook.

Abbreviations
Crochet abbreviations appear on page 22.

SHAMROCK BORDER *(blue)*

Work 21ch.

FOUNDATION ROW 1tr into 8th ch from hook, [2ch, miss 2ch, 1tr into next ch] 3 times, 5ch, miss 3ch, [1tr, 3ch] 3 times into next ch, 1tr into same ch, 1ch, turn.

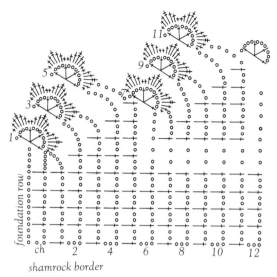

shamrock border

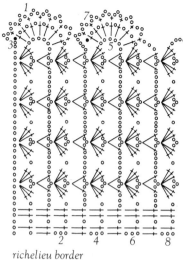

richelieu border

O   *ch*

+   *dc*

†   *htr*

†   *tr*

‡   *dtr*

●   *ss*

ROW 1 [1dc, 1htr, 1tr, 1dtr, 1tr, 1htr, 1dc] into each of next three 3ch sps (shamrock made), 5ch, 1tr into 5ch lp (on future repeats, this will be a 7ch lp), [2ch, 1tr into next tr] 4 times, 2ch, miss 2ch, 1tr into next ch, 5ch, turn.

ROW 2 1tr into next tr, [2ch, 1tr into next tr] 4 times, 2ch, 1tr into 5ch lp, 7ch, [1tr, 3ch] 3 times into dtr at centre of second petal, 1tr into same place, 1ch, turn.

ROW 3 Make shamrock as before, 5ch, 1tr into 7ch lp, * 2ch, 1tr into next tr; rep from * to end, working last tr into 3rd of 5ch, 5ch, turn.

ROW 4 Rep row 2, but work [2ch, 1tr into next tr] 6 times instead of 4 times.

ROW 5 Rep row 3.

ROW 6 1tr into next tr, [2ch, 1tr into next tr] 3 times, 7ch, miss 4sps, [1tr, 3ch] 3 times into next sp, 1tr into same sp, 1ch, turn.

Repeat rows 1 to 6, ending with a 5th row.

RICHELIEU BORDER (peach)
Work 35ch.

FOUNDATION ROW 1tr into 3rd ch from hook, 1ch, miss 1ch, 1tr into each of next 2ch, 1ch, miss 3ch, 3tr into next ch, 3ch, 3tr into next ch, [1ch, miss 5ch, 3tr into next ch, 3ch, 3tr into next ch] 3 times, leave last 3ch unworked, 6ch, turn.

ROW 1 [1tr, 3ch, 1tr] into 3ch lp, [5ch, (1tr, 3ch, 1tr) into next 3ch lp] 3 times, 3ch, 1tr into each of next 2tr, 1ch, 1tr into last tr, 1tr into 3rd of 6ch, 3ch, turn.

ROW 2 1tr into next tr, 1ch, 1tr into each of next 2tr, [1ch, (3tr, 3ch, 3tr) into 3ch lp] 4 times, [1ch, 1tr] 7 times into 3ch lp, ss to last ch of foundation row.

* Note that in future repeats, the ss at the end of row 2 is worked into the 3ch lp of the previous pattern.

ROW 3 [3ch, 1dc into 1ch sp] 7 times, 3ch, [1tr, 3ch, 1tr] into 3ch sp, [5ch, (1tr, 3ch, 1tr) into 3ch lp] 3 times, 3ch, 1tr into each of next 2tr, 1ch, 1tr into next tr, 1tr into turning ch, 3ch, turn.

ROW 4 1tr into next tr, 1ch, 1tr into each of next 2tr, [1ch (3tr, 3ch, 3tr) into 3ch lp] 4 times, 6ch, turn.

Repeat rows 1 to 4.

SQUARE CROCHET MOTIFS

Abbreviations
Crochet abbreviations appear on page 22.

Special abbreviation for Afghan square: 1cl (1 cluster) = ** yarn round hook (yrh), insert hook into ring, yarn round hook, draw loop through, yarn round hook, draw loop through 2 loops **, repeat from ** to ** 3 times more, yarn round hook, draw loop through 4 loops.

OLD AMERICA (mauve and white)
Using light coloured yarn, work 6ch and join with ss to form a ring.

ROUND 1 (Light) 3ch (counts as 1tr), 2tr into ring, 3ch, * 3tr into ring, 3ch; rep

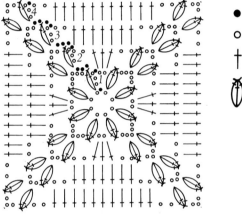

into each corner sp; cont from * to end, ending with 1ch, ss into 3rd of 3ch. Break off yarn.

ROUND 4 (Dark) Join yarn to corner sp, 3ch, [2tr, 3ch, 3tr] into same sp, * 1ch, 3tr into each 1ch sp, 1ch, [3tr, 3ch, 3tr] into each corner sp; cont from * to end, ending with 1ch, ss into 3rd of 3ch. Break off yarn.

AFGHAN SQUARE (beige)

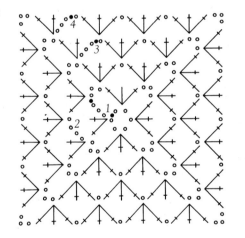

- ● *ss*
- ○ *ch*
- ✝ *tr*
- ✖ *cluster (cl)*

Work 8ch; join with ss to form ring.
ROUND 1 3ch, ** yrh, insert hook into ring, yrh, draw lp through, yrh, draw through 2 lps **, rep from ** to **, yrh, draw through 3lps, 5ch, * 1cl, 2ch, 1cl, 5ch; rep from * twice more, 1cl, 2ch, join with ss into 3rd of 3ch.
ROUND 2 Ss into 5ch sp, 3ch, rep from ** to ** twice, yrh, draw through 3lps, 2ch, 1cl into same sp, * 2ch, 3tr into 2ch sp, 2ch, [1cl, 2ch, 1cl] into 5ch sp, rep from * twice more, 2ch, 3tr into 2ch sp, 2ch, join with ss to 3rd of 3ch.
ROUND 3 Ss into corner 2ch sp, 3ch, rep from ** to ** twice, yrh, draw through 3lps, 2ch, 1cl into same sp, * 2ch, 2tr into 2ch sp, 1tr into each of next 3tr, 2tr into 2ch sp, 2ch, [1cl, 2ch, 1cl] into corner 2ch sp, rep from * twice more, 2ch, 2tr into 2ch sp, 1tr into each of next 3tr, 2tr into 2ch sp, 2ch, join with ss to 3rd of 3ch.

Square crochet motifs are internationally popular, from the traditional Old America design (shown here in mauve and white) to the modern Afghan square (see the beige example).
All the designs can be worked in several colours, by simply breaking off the yarn at the end of each round and joining in another colour, but they look equally effective worked in a single colour.

from * twice more, ss into 3rd of 3ch. Break off yarn.
ROUND 2 (Dark) Join yarn to 3ch sp, 3ch, [2tr, 3ch, 3tr] into same sp, * 1ch, [3 tr, 3ch, 3tr] into next 3ch sp; rep from * twice more, ss into 3rd of 3ch. Break yarn.
ROUND 3 (Light) Join yarn to corner sp, 3ch, [2tr, 3ch, 3tr] into same sp, * 1ch, 3tr into each 1ch sp, 1ch, [3tr, 3ch, 3tr]

ROUND 4 Rep round 3, but working 1tr into each of 7tr instead of 3tr along each side.

Cont in this way, working 4 more tr along each side in each round until square is required size.
Fasten off.

FRAMED SUN *(green)*

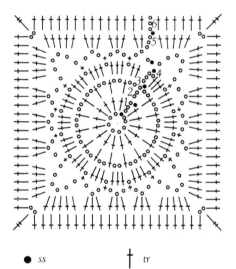

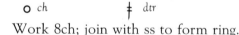

•	ss	
o	ch	

Work 8ch; join with ss to form ring.

ROUND 1 3ch (counts as 1tr), work 15tr into ring, ss to 3rd of 3ch.

ROUND 2 5ch (counts as 1tr, 2ch), [1tr into next tr, 2ch] 15 times, ss to 3rd of 5ch.

ROUND 3 3ch, 2tr into first sp, 1ch, [3tr, 1ch] into each sp, ss to 3rd of 3ch.

ROUND 4 * [3ch, 1dc into next 1ch sp] 3 times, 6ch, 1dc into next sp; cont from * to end, ss to first of 3ch.

ROUND 5 3ch, 2tr into first 3ch sp, 3tr into each of next two 3ch sps, * [5tr, 2ch, 5tr] into each corner sp, 3tr into each 3ch sp; cont from * to end, join with ss to 3rd of 3ch.

ROUND 6 3ch, work 1tr into each st and [1tr, 1dtr, 1tr] into each 2ch corner sp.
Fasten off.

ST GEORGE SQUARE *(peach)*

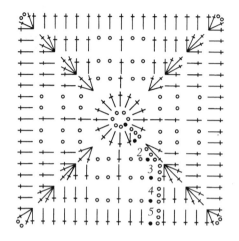

Work 6ch. Join with ss to form ring.
ROUND 1 3ch (counts as 1tr), work 15tr into ring, join with ss into 3rd of 3ch.
ROUND 2 3ch (counts as 1tr), 2tr into same st as last ss, 2ch, miss 1tr, 1tr into next tr, 2ch, miss 1tr, * 3tr into next tr, 2ch, miss 1tr, 1tr into next tr, 2ch, miss 1tr; rep from * twice, join with ss into 3rd of 3ch.
ROUND 3 3ch, 5tr into next tr, * 1tr into next tr, [2ch, 1tr into next tr] twice, 5tr into next tr; rep from * twice, [1tr into next tr, 2ch] twice, join with ss into 3rd of 3ch.
ROUND 4 3ch, 1tr into each of next 2tr, 5tr into next tr, * 1tr into each of next 3tr, 2ch, 1tr into next tr, 2ch, 1tr into each of next 3tr, 5tr into next tr; rep from * twice, 1tr into each of next 3tr, 2ch, 1tr into next tr, 2ch, join with ss into 3rd of 3ch.
ROUND 5 3ch, 1tr into each of next 4tr, [2tr, 2ch, 2tr] into next tr, * 1tr into each of next 5tr, 2tr into next 2ch sp, 1tr into next tr, 2tr into next 2ch sp, 1tr into each of next 5tr, [2tr, 2ch, 2tr] into next tr; rep from * twice, 1tr into each of next 5tr, 2tr into next 2ch sp, 1tr into next tr, 2tr into last ch sp, join with ss to 3rd of 3ch. Fasten off.

HEXAGONAL CROCHET MOTIFS

Abbreviations

Crochet abbreviations appear on page 22. Special abbrev. for popcorn motif:

popcorn = work 5 trebles into next stitch, drop loop from hook, insert hook into top of first of these trebles, pick up dropped loop and draw through, work 1 chain to secure popcorn.

picot = work 3 chain then work slip stitch into first of these chain.

CLEMATIS HEXAGON (cream)

Work 6ch. Join with ss to form ring.

ROUND 1 1ch, 12dc into ring, ss to first dc.
ROUND 2 1ch, 1dc into same place as 1ch, [7ch, miss 1dc, 1dc into next dc] 5 times, 3ch, miss 1dc, 1dtr into top of first dc.
ROUND 3 3ch (counts as 1tr), 4tr into lp formed by dtr, [3ch, 5tr into next 7ch lp] 5 times, 3ch, ss into 3rd of 3ch.
ROUND 4 3ch (counts as 1tr), 1tr into each of next 4tr, * 3ch, 1dc into next 3ch sp, 3ch **, 1tr into each of next 5tr; rep from * 4 times more and then from * to ** once again, ss to 3rd of 3ch.
ROUND 5 3ch, tr4tog over next 4tr (counts as tr5tog), * [5ch, 1dc into next 3ch sp] twice, 5ch **, tr5tog over next 5tr; rep from * 4 times and then from * to ** once again, ss into top of tr4tog.
ROUND 6 Ss into each of next 3ch, 1ch, 1dc into same place, * 5ch, 1dc into next 5ch sp; rep from * to end, omitting last dc and ending with ss into first dc.
ROUND 7 Ss into each of next 3ch, 1ch, 1dc into same place, * 5ch, 1dc into next 5ch sp, 3ch, [5tr, 3ch, 5tr] into next sp, 3ch, 1dc into next sp; rep from * 5 more times, omitting last dc and ending with ss into first dc.
Fasten off.

Hexagonal motifs fit together neatly without the addition of smaller joining motifs. The three designs shown here can be worked in thick cotton, wool or synthetic yarns to make bedspreads, blankets, cushion covers, shawls and wraps, using just one colour such as white or a rainbow of coordinating shades.

clematis hexagon

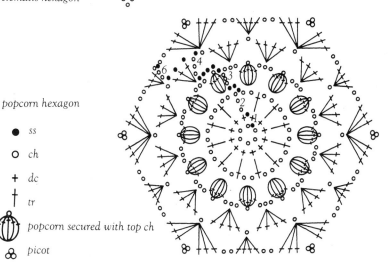

popcorn hexagon

- ● ss
- ○ ch
- + dc
- † tr
- popcorn secured with top ch
- picot

FLOWER HEXAGON *(mauve)*
Work 6ch. Join with ss to form a ring.

ROUND 1 4ch (counts as 1tr, 1ch), [1tr into ring, 1ch] 11 times, join with ss to 3rd of 4ch.

ROUND 2 3ch (counts as 1tr), 2tr into 1ch sp, 1tr into next tr, 2ch, * 1tr into next tr, 2tr into 1ch sp, 1tr into next tr, 2ch; rep from * 4 times more, join with ss to 3rd of 3ch.

ROUND 3 3ch, 1tr into same place, 1tr into each of next 2tr, 2tr into next tr, 2ch, * 2tr into next tr, 1tr into each of next 2tr, 2tr into next tr, 2ch; rep from * 4 times, join with ss to 3rd of 3ch.

ROUND 4 3ch, 1tr into same place, 1tr into each of next 4tr, 2tr into next tr, 2ch, * 2tr into next tr, 1tr into each of next 4tr, 2tr into next tr, 2ch; rep from *4 times more, join with ss to 3rd of 3ch.

ROUND 5 3ch, 1tr into each of next 7tr, * 3ch, 1 dc into 2ch sp, 3ch, 1tr into each of next 8tr; rep from * 4 times more, 3ch, 1dc into 2ch sp, 3ch, join with ss to 3rd of 3ch.

ROUND 6 Ss into next tr, 3ch, 1tr into each of next 5tr, * 3ch, [1dc into 3ch sp, 3ch] twice, miss next tr, 1tr into each of next 6tr; rep from * 4 times more, 3ch, [1dc into 3ch sp, 3ch] twice, join with ss to 3rd of 3ch.

ROUND 7 Ss into next tr, 3ch, 1tr into each of next 3tr, * 3ch, [1dc into 3ch sp, 3ch] 3 times, miss next tr, 1tr into each of next 4tr; rep from * 4 times more, 3ch, [1 dc into 3ch sp, 3ch] 3 times, join with ss to 3rd of 3ch.

ROUND 8 Ss between 2nd and 3rd tr of group, 3ch (counts as 1tr), 1tr into same place, * 3ch, [1dc into 3ch sp, 3ch] 4 times, 2tr between 2nd and 3rd tr of group; rep from * 4 times more, 3ch, [1dc into 3ch sp, 3ch] 4 times, join with ss to 3rd of 3ch.
Fasten off.

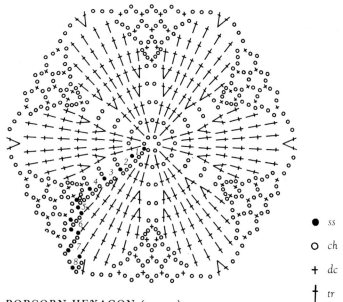

● ss

○ ch

+ dc

† tr

POPCORN HEXAGON *(green)*
Work 6ch and join with ss to form a ring.

ROUND 1 1ch, work 12dc into ring, join with ss into first dc.

ROUND 2 5ch (counts as 1tr, 2ch), miss first dc, [1tr into next dc, 2ch] 11 times, join with ss into 3rd of 5ch.

ROUND 3 Ss into first 2ch sp, 3ch, 4tr into same sp as ss, drop loop from hook, insert hook into top of 3ch, pick up dropped loop and draw through, 1ch to secure (counts as first popcorn), 3ch, [1 popcorn into next 2ch sp, 3ch] 11 times, join with ss into top of first popcorn.

ROUND 4 Ss into first 3ch sp, 3ch (counts as 1tr), 3tr into same sp as ss, 1ch, [4tr into next 3ch sp, 1ch] 11 times, join with ss to 3rd of 3ch.

ROUND 5 Ss into each of next 3tr and into next ch sp, 3ch, 3tr into same sp as last ss, 2ch, [3tr, 1 picot, 3tr] into next ch sp, * 2ch, 4tr into next ch sp, 2ch, [3tr, 1 picot, 3tr] into next ch sp; rep from * 4 times more, 2ch, join with ss to 3rd of 3ch.
Fasten off.

CIRCULAR CROCHET MOTIFS

Abbreviations
Crochet abbreviations appear on page 22.

TINY ROSE (blue)

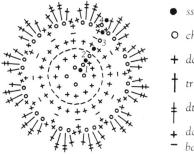

- ● ss
- ○ ch
- + dc
- † tr
- ‡ dtr
- + dc through
- − back loop

Work 4ch. Join with ss to form ring.

ROUND 1 1ch, 12dc into ring, join with ss to first ch.

ROUND 2 1ch, 2dc into each dc (inserting hook into back loop of each st), join with ss to first ch.

ROUND 3 1ch, * 1dc into next dc (inserting hook into back loop of st), 2ch, miss 1dc; rep from * to end, join with ss to first ch.

ROUND 4 1ch, * [1dc, 1tr, 2dtr, 1tr, 1dc] into next 2ch sp; rep from * to end, join with ss to first ch. Fasten off.

ELIZABETHAN FLOWER (pink)
Work 8ch. Join with ss to form a ring.

ROUND 1 6ch (counts as 1tr, 3ch), [1tr into ring, 3ch] 7 times, join with ss to 3rd of 6ch.

ROUND 2 3ch (counts as 1tr), 5tr into first 3ch sp, [6tr into next 3ch sp] 7 times, join with ss to 3rd of 3ch.

ROUND 3 3ch, 1tr into each of next 5tr (inserting hook into back loop of each st), 3ch, [1tr into each of next 6tr (inserting hook into back loop of each st), 3ch] 7 times, join with ss to 3rd of 3ch.

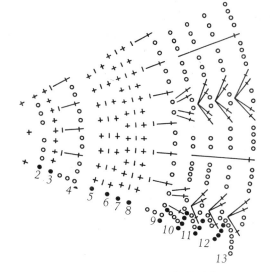

- ● ss
- ○ ch
- + dc
- † tr
- + dc through back loop
- ‡ dc around previous three rounds 6ch lps

ROUND 4 4ch (counts as 1dtr), 1dtr into each of next 5tr leaving last lp of each dtr on hook (6 loops on hook), [yrh, pull through 3 lps] twice, yrh, pull through 2 lps, 8ch, 1dc into 3ch sp, 8ch, * 1dtr into each of next 6tr leaving last lp on hook (7 lps on hook), [yrh, pull through 3 lps] 3 times, 8ch, 1dc into 3ch sp, 8ch; rep from * 6 times more, join with ss to top of first dtr group.

ROUND 5 [9dc into next 8ch sp] 16 times, join with ss to first dc. Fasten off.

Work small motifs, such as the tiny rose shown in blue, in fine, metallic yarn. One motif could decorate a knitted garment, or several could hang on a Christmas tree.

Larger designs, like the snowflake circle, can be worked in thick cotton yarn and used on its own as a mat to protect a polished table top.

SNOWFLAKE CIRCLE (*peach*)
Work 10ch and join with ss to form a ring.

ROUND 1 24dc into ring, ss into first dc.
ROUND 2 [6ch, miss 2dc, 1dc into next dc] 8 times, ss into first ch.
ROUND 3 [8dc into next 6ch sp] 8 times, ss into first dc.
ROUND 4 5ch (counts as 1tr, 2ch), miss 1dc, * 1tr into back loop of next dc, 2ch, miss 1dc; rep from * to end, ss into 3rd of 5ch.
ROUND 5 [2dc into next 2ch sp] to end, ss into first dc.
(64dc)
ROUND 6 1dc into back loop of each dc to end, ss into first dc.
ROUND 7 Working into both loops of each st, [2dc into next dc, 1dc into next dc] to end.
(96dc)
ROUND 8 Rep round 6.
ROUND 9 Rep round 4.
ROUND 10 Ss into next 2ch sp, 3ch (counts as 1tr), 1tr into same sp, 2ch, 2tr into same sp, * 6ch, miss two 2ch sps, [2tr, 2ch, 2tr] into next 2ch sp; rep from * ending 6ch, ss into 3rd of 3ch.
(16tr groups)
ROUND 11 Ss into next 2ch sp, 3ch (counts as 1tr), 1tr into same sp, 2ch, 2tr into same sp, 6ch, * [2tr, 2ch, 2tr] into next 2ch sp, 6ch; rep from * to end, ss into 3rd of 3ch.
ROUND 12 Rep round 11.
ROUND 13 Ss into next 2ch sp, 3ch, 1tr into same sp, 2ch, 2tr into same sp, 4ch, insert hook under three 6ch lps of previous 3 rounds and work 1dc to enclose ch lps, 4ch, * [2tr, 2ch, 2tr] into next 2ch sp, 4ch, 1dc to enclose ch lps as before, 4ch; rep from * to end, ss into 3rd of 3ch.
Fasten off.

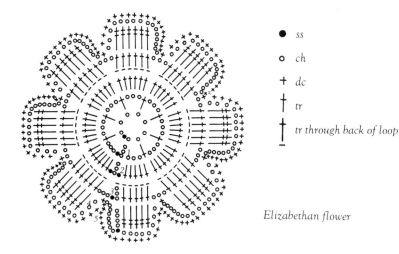

●	ss
○	ch
+	dc
†	tr
‡	tr through back of loop

Elizabethan flower

OPENWORK PATTERNS

Abbreviations
Crochet abbreviations appear on page 22.
Abbreviation for lattice stripes: puff st = [yarn over hook, draw through a loop] 3 times, yarn over hook and draw through all 7 loops on hook, 1 chain to finish.

SHADOWS AND SPACES (*blue*)
Work a multiple of 6ch plus 3.
FOUNDATION ROW Work 1tr into 4th ch from hook, 1tr into each ch to end, 3ch, turn.
ROW 1 1tr into next st, * 3ch, miss 3 sts, 1tr into each of next 3 sts; rep from * to

Three of the patterns, shown in cream, pink and beige, are perfect for working in fine two and three ply wool or synthetic yarns to make light, summery wraps and square shawls. The fourth pattern, shown in blue, is best worked in fine or medium-weight cotton yarn and would make an unusual café-style curtain.

end, ending with 1tr into last st, 1tr into top of turning ch, turn.

ROW 2 * 3tr into 3ch sp, 3ch; rep from * to end, ending with 1ch, 1tr into top of turning ch, 3ch, turn.

ROW 3 1tr into 1ch sp, * 3ch, 3tr into 3ch sp; rep from * to end, ending with 2tr into turning ch, 3ch, turn.

ROW 4 1tr into each ch and st to end of row, 3ch, turn.

ROW 5 1tr into each st to end, 3ch, turn.

ROW 6 Rep row 5.

Repeat rows 1 to 6.

BAR AND LATTICE (beige)

Work a multiple of 4ch plus 6.

FOUNDATION ROW 1tr into 10th ch from hook, * 3ch, miss 3ch, 1tr into next ch; rep from * to end, 4ch, turn.

ROW 1 * 1dc into 2nd of 3ch, 2ch, 1tr into next tr, 2ch; rep from * to end, ending with 1dc into 2nd ch, 2ch, 1tr into turning ch, 5ch, turn.

ROW 2 1tr into next tr, * 3ch, 1tr into next tr; rep from * to end, working last tr into turning ch, 4ch, turn.

Repeat rows 1 and 2.

FANCY TRELLIS (cream)

Work a multiple of 4ch plus 6.

FOUNDATION ROW Work [1dc, 3ch, 1dc] into 6th ch from hook, * 5ch, miss 3ch, [1dc, 3ch, 1dc] into next ch; rep from * to end, ending with 1dc into last ch, 5ch, turn.

ROW 1 * [1dc, 3ch, 1dc] into 3rd ch of 5ch lp, 5ch; rep from * to end, ending with 5ch, 1dc into turning ch, 5ch, turn.

Repeat row 1.

LATTICE STRIPES (pink)

Work a multiple of 8ch plus 2.

FOUNDATION ROW Work 1dc into 2nd ch from hook, * 2ch, miss 3ch, [1tr, 3ch, 1tr] into next ch, 2ch, miss 3ch, 1dc into next ch; rep from * to end, 6ch, turn.

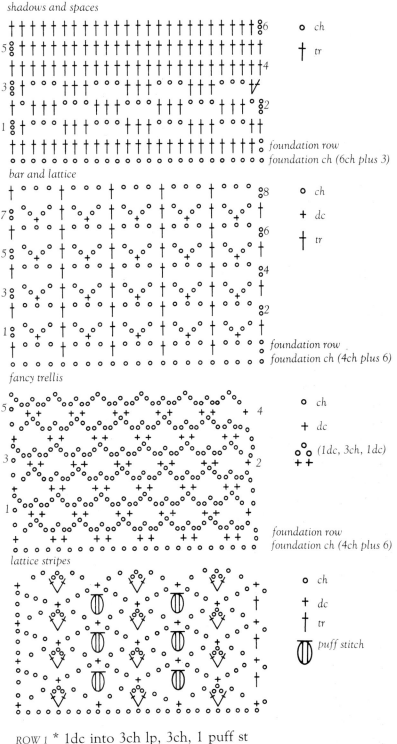

shadows and spaces

○ ch
† tr

foundation row
foundation ch (6ch plus 3)

bar and lattice

○ ch
+ dc
† tr

foundation row
foundation ch (4ch plus 6)

fancy trellis

○ ch
+ dc
(1dc, 3ch, 1dc)

foundation row
foundation ch (4ch plus 6)

lattice stripes

○ ch
+ dc
† tr
puff stitch

ROW 1 * 1dc into 3ch lp, 3ch, 1 puff st into dc, 3ch; rep from * to end, ending with 1tr into last dc, 1ch, turn.

ROW 2 1dc into first st, * 2ch, [1tr, 3ch, 1tr] into next dc, 2ch, 1dc into top of puff st; rep from * to end, ending with 1dc into turning ch, 6ch, turn.

Repeat rows 1 and 2.

SHELL STITCHES

Abbreviations

Crochet abbreviations appear on page 22.

LARGE SHELLS (cream)

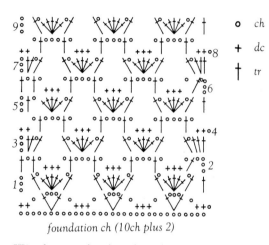

o ch
+ dc
† tr

foundation ch (10ch plus 2)

Work a multiple of 10ch plus 2.

FOUNDATION ROW Work 1dc into first ch from hook, 1dc into next ch, * 1ch, miss 3ch, [1tr, 3ch, 1tr] into next ch, 1ch, miss 3ch, 1dc into each of next 3ch; rep from * to end, ending with 1dc into each of last 2ch, 3ch, turn.

ROW 1 * 1tr into first tr, 1ch, 5tr into 3ch sp, 1ch, 1tr into last tr of group; rep from * to end, ending with 1tr into last st, 4ch, turn.

ROW 2 * 1tr into first tr of group, 1ch, 1dc into each of centre 3 sts, 1ch, 1tr into last tr of group, 3ch; rep from * to end, ending with 1ch, 1tr into turning ch, 3ch, turn.

ROW 3 2tr into 1ch sp, 1ch, 1tr into next st, * 1tr into first tr of next group, 1ch, 5tr into 3ch sp, 1ch, 1tr into last tr of group; rep from * to end, ending with 1tr into last tr, 1ch, 3tr into turning ch, 1ch, turn.

ROW 4 1dc into first st, 1dc into next st, 1ch, 1tr into next tr, * 3ch, 1tr into first tr of group, 1ch, 1dc into each of centre 3 sts, 1ch, 1tr into last st of group; rep from * to end, ending with 1dc into last st, 1dc into turning ch, 3ch, turn.

Repeat rows 1 to 4.

VENETIAN SHELLS (green)

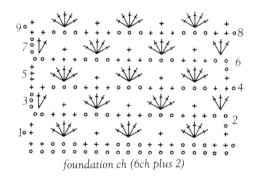

foundation ch (6ch plus 2)

Work a multiple of 6ch plus 2.

FOUNDATION ROW 1dc into 2nd ch from hook, 1dc into next ch, * 3ch, miss 3ch, 1dc into each of next 3ch; rep from * to last 5ch, 3ch, miss 3ch, 1dc into each of last 2ch, 1ch, turn.

ROW 1 1dc into first dc, * 5tr into 3ch sp, miss 1dc, 1dc into next dc; rep from * to end, 3ch, turn.

ROW 2 * 1dc into 2nd, 3rd and 4th of 5tr group, 3ch; rep from * to end, ending with 1dc into 2nd, 3rd and 4th of 5tr

Shell stitches are quick and easy to work and create a very attractive result whether the shells are arranged in vertical rows, as in the beige example, or alternately, like the green example. Work shell stitches in fine, soft yarns to make lacy shawls, and baby clothes, or in heavier weight wool or cotton for household items.

group, 2ch, 1dc into last st, 3ch, turn.
ROW 3 2tr into 2ch sp, miss 1dc, 1dc into next dc, * 5tr into 3ch sp, miss 1dc, 1dc into next dc; rep from * to end, 3tr into last ch sp, 1ch, turn.
ROW 4 1dc into each of first 2tr, * 3ch, 1dc into 2nd, 3rd and 4th of 5tr group; rep from * to end, ending with 3ch, 1dc into each of last 2tr, 1ch, turn.
Repeat rows 1 to 4.

SHELL STRIPES (beige)

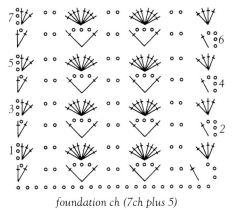

foundation ch (7ch plus 5)

Work a multiple of 7ch plus 5.
FOUNDATION ROW Work 1tr into 5th ch from hook, * 2ch, miss 6ch, [1tr, 3ch, 1tr] into next ch; rep from * to end, ending with [1tr, 1ch, 1tr] into last ch, 3ch, turn.
ROW 1 3tr into 1ch sp, * 8tr into 3ch sp; rep from * to end, ending with 5tr into turning ch, 4ch, turn.
ROW 2 1tr into first st, * 2ch, [1tr, 3ch, 1tr] into space between 4th and 5th sts of group; rep from * to end, ending [1tr, 1ch, 1tr] into last st, 3ch, turn.
Repeat rows 1 and 2.

TINY SHELLS (pink)

Work a multiple of 6ch plus 4.
FOUNDATION ROW [1tr, 2ch, 1tr] into 7th ch from hook, * miss 2ch, [2tr, 1ch, 2tr] into next ch, miss 2ch, [1tr, 2ch, 1tr] into next ch; rep from * to last 3ch, miss 2ch, 1tr into last ch, 3ch, turn.

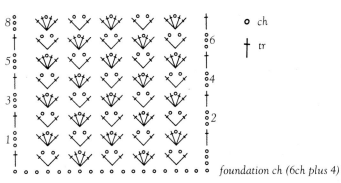

o ch
† tr

foundation ch (6ch plus 4)

ROW 1 * [2tr, 1ch, 1tr] into 2ch sp, [1tr, 2ch, 1tr] into 1ch sp; rep from * to end, ending with [2tr, 1ch, 2tr] into 2ch sp, 1tr into turning ch, 3ch, turn.
ROW 2 * [1tr, 2ch, 1tr] into 1ch sp, [2tr, 1ch, 2tr] into 2ch sp; rep from * to end, ending with [1tr, 2ch, 1tr] into 1ch sp, 1tr into turning ch, 3ch, turn.
Repeat rows 1 and 2.

FILET CROCHET MOTIFS

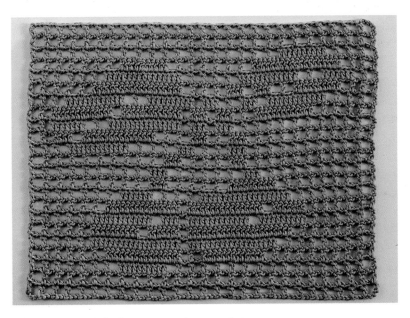

These pictorial charts can be used in a variety of ways. Small motifs worked in fine yarn make pincushions and sachets. Other designs can be worked in thicker cotton for cushion covers or tablemats.

As well as altering the size, different yarns will affect the final appearance – fine yarns give a lacy look, while heavy yarns produce a more substantial piece.

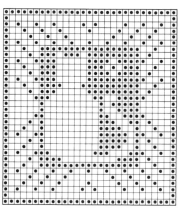

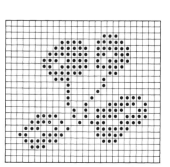

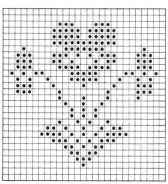

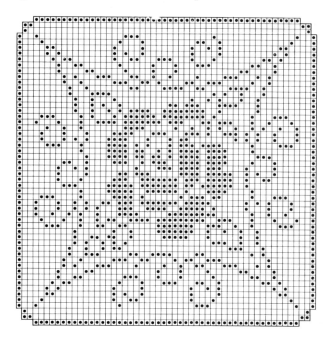

FILET CROCHET INSERTIONS AND BORDERS

This selection of charts for filet crochet insertions and borders gives you pictorial designs and abstract designs. All are worked widthways which means you simply work at a strip until it is the right length for your needs, remembering to finish working at the end of a repeat, so the pattern at both ends of the strip will match.

Use insertions between two pieces of fabric to decorate tablecloths or bedlinen, while the borders can edge anything.

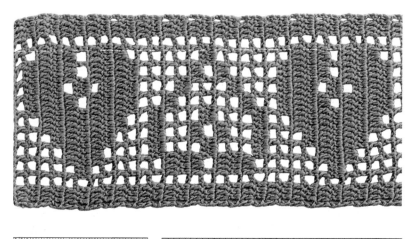

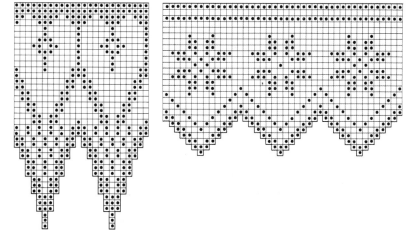

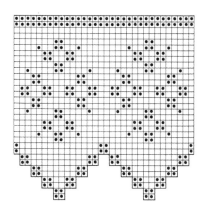
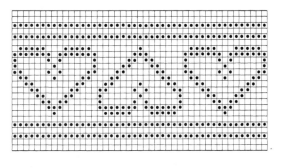
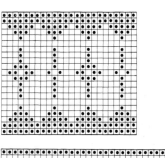
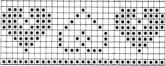

FILET CROCHET ALPHABET

This alphabet can be used to decorate many crochet items from personalized borders for bath towels, to larger pieces such as cushion covers and pictures which spell out a name or greeting.

First work out your designs on graph paper, then work up a small sample piece before beginning on the complete project. You will find full instructions on page 21 showing how to make your own chart and how to work from a chart.

■ block
□ space

USEFUL SUPPLIERS

Aladdins Cave
West Side Centre
1 West St
Kempton Park 1619
South Africa
(011) 975 3120

Arthur Bales
Biccard St
Braamfontein
Johannesburg 2001
South Africa
(011) 339 3268
and
62 4th Avenue
Linden
Johannesburg 2195
South Africa
(011) 888 2401

Busy Hands
Atlasville Centre
Finch Rd
Atlasville
Boksburg 1459
South Africa
(011) 395 1065

Dot's Wool and Handcraft
2 Hatfield Plaza
1131 Park St
Hatfield
Pretoria 0083
South Africa
(012) 43 2455

Harriett Habbs
6 Park 'n Shop
Meadowridge
Cape Town 7800
South Africa
(021) 724140

Knitting Wool Centre
122 Victoria Rd
Woodstock
Cape Town 7925
South Africa
(021) 47 1134
and
20C Durban Rd
Bellville 7530
South Africa
(021) 948 8077
and
235 Meyer St
Germiston 1401
South Africa
(011) 825 5366

Orion Knitting Supplies
Groote Kerk Arcade
32 Parliament St
Cape Town 8001
South Africa
(021) 461 6941

Pied Piper
41 Parliament St
Emerald Hill
Port Elizabeth 6011
South Africa
(041) 52 3090

Petit Point Wool and
Handicrafts
Tyger Valley Centre
Willie van Schoor Ave
Bellville 7530
South Africa
(021) 948 2335

The Wool and Baby Centre
208 Commercial Rd
Pietermaritzberg 3201
South Africa
(0331) 94 5577

Woolworld International
332 Victoria Rd
Salt River
Cape Town 7925
South Africa
(021) 448 4004
and
133 Voortrekker Rd
Parow
Cape Town 7500
South Africa
(021) 930 1270

Wynberg Wool Shop
48 Church Street
Wynberg
Cape Town 7800
(021) 761 4758

GLOSSARY

Ball band – the paper strip around a ball of yarn giving weight, colour and dye lot numbers, fibre content and care instructions. May also contain other details.

Blocking – setting the pattern by stretching and pinning out a piece of damp crochet and allowing it to dry.

Border – a *deep* strip of patterned crochet with one straight and one shaped edge. Usually worked in short rows across the width.

Chart – pattern instructions expressed as symbols.

Crochet pattern – complete instructions showing how to make a crochet article.

Dye lot – the batch of dye used for a specific ball of yarn. Shades can vary between batches, so use yarn from the same batch to make one item.

Edging – a *narrow* strip of patterned crochet with one straight and one shaped edge. Usually worked in short rows across the width.

Filet crochet – patterned crochet worked from a grid chart. The pattern elements are worked solidly and set against a regularly-worked openwork background.

Foundation chain (also called foundation row) – a length of chain stitches which forms the base row for a piece of crochet.

Insertion – a strip of patterned crochet with parallel edges. Usually worked in short rows across the width.

Mercerizing – process for cotton which produces a strong, lustrous finish.

Motif – a shaped piece of crochet worked in rounds which can be joined together rather like fabric patchwork to make a larger piece.

Pattern repeat – the specific number of rows which are needed to complete one stitch pattern.

Ply – the number of strands which are twisted together to make a yarn.

Starch a natural or synthetic substance used for stiffening crochet or lace.

Starting chain – a specific number of chain worked at the beginning of a *round* to bring the hook up to the correct height for the crochet stitch which is being worked.

Stitch pattern – a sequence of stitches needed to create a specific design, expressed as row-by-row (or round-by-round) instructions, either written or charted.

Tapestry needle – a blunt embroidery needle with a long, large eye.

Tension – the looseness or tightness of a crochet fabric generally expressed as a specific number of rows and stitches in a given area, usually 10 cm (4 in) square.

Turning chain – a specific number of chain worked at the beginning of a *row* to bring the hook up to the correct height for the stitch which is being worked.

BIBLIOGRAPHY

D'Arcy, Eithne, *Irish Crochet Lace*, Colin Smythe, 1990

Klickman, Flora, *The Home Art Crochet Book*, Dover, 1990

Rabun Ough, Anne, *New Directions in Crochet*, David & Charles, 1981

Rankin, Chris, *Victorian Country Lace*, Anaya, 1990

Index

A

abbreviations 22
Afghan square motif 67
alphabets 77
aluminium hooks 12
angora 11
Aran weight yarn 10
asterisks 23

B

bags 54, 59
ball band 12, 19
ball sizes 11
bars 9, 21, 22
bedspreads 28, 36, 42
blocking 26
bone hooks 7
borders 14, 24, 28, 65, 66, 76
brackets 23
braid, crochet 64
Branchardiere, Eleanore Riego de la 7
bulky yarn 10
butterfly motif 39

C

Carrickmacross lace 8
chain stitch 8, 16, 18
charts, how to follow 24
Christmas stars 62
chunky yarn 10
circular motifs 71, 72
clematis hexagon motif 71, 72
Clones lace 8
conversion chart, hooks 11
crossed double stitch 18

D

double crochet 9, 10, 16
double-double 10
double knitting yarn 10
double treble stitch 10, 17
dyes 12

E

edgings 14, 15, 24, 28, 64, 65
Edwardian fence edging 65

F

4-ply yarn 10
filet crochet 8, 9, 21, 22, 24, 39, 75

insertions and borders 76
fingering yarn 10
finishing techniques 26–28
fisherman yarn 10
flower hexagon motif 60, 70
foundation chain 18, 19

G

garments 15
gauge, see tension
Godey's Lady's Book 8

H

half double stitch 10
half treble stitch 10, 17
hanks 11
heavyweight yarn 10
hexagon motifs 59, 60, 61, 69, 70
hooks 7, 9, 10, 11, 12
   conversion chart 11
home furnishings 15

IJ

insertions 14, 29, 76
Irish crochet lace 8
Italian crochet lace 7
ivory hooks 7
joining
   a new ball 20
   motifs 26–27

L

lacets 9, 21, 22
lattice stripes pattern 73
lavender 59
lightweight yarn 10

M

markers 14
mohair 11
motifs 20, 24, 26, 27, 36, 39, 45, 66–76

N

Needle, The 8
nun's lace 7

O

Old America pattern 66
origins 6
oversewing 26, 27

P

pattern library 64–79
   how to use 24
patterns, how to follow 23
pincushions 51
pinning out 26
pins 14, 26, 28
plastic hooks 12
popcorn hexagon motif 30

R

repairs 29
repeats 15, 23
Richelieu border 66
rose motifs 8, 39, 51, 71
rounds 19, 20
row counter 15, 23

S

St George square 68
sewing needles 14, 28
scalloped edging 64
scissors 14
shadows and spaces pattern 72
shamrock border 65
shamrock motif 8
shelf edgings 48
shell stitches 64
   Venetian shells 74
   stripes 75
shepherd's knitting 7
single crochet stitch 10
skeins 11
slip stitch 16, 20, 27
snowflake motifs 45, 72
sport, yarn 10
square motifs 66–68
stains 29
starch 29
star motifs 62
steel hooks 12, 14
stitches 16–18
storing crochet lace 29
sun, framed motif 68
symbols 24

T

3 ply yarn 10
tablecloths 32, 39
table-linen 29
tape measure 14
tapestry needles 14, 20, 28
tension 10, 15, 16
threads 14
towels 32
traycloth 45

treble crochet stitch (US) 10
treble stitch 9, 10, 17
trellis 73
Tunisian crochet 6
turning chains 19

U

US terms 10

W

washing crochet lace 29
Weldon's Practical Crochet 8
windmill hexagon motif 60
Woman's Magazine 8
wooden hooks 14
wool, see yarns
worsted yarn 10

Y

yarns 6, 9, 15
   calculating requirements 15
   choosing and using 11–12